Real Estate Secrets

Real Estate Secrets

✦

From Foreclosures to eBay.

Alex and Rhonda Reid

iUniverse, Inc.
New York Lincoln Shanghai

Real Estate Secrets
From Foreclosures to eBay.

iUniverse books may be ordered through booksellers or by contacting:

iUniverse
2021 Pine Lake Road, Suite 100
Lincoln, NE 68512
www.iuniverse.com
1-800-Authors (1-800-288-4677)

This publication is only meant to be used for educational and informative purposes. Before making any decisions you should consult with a professional who understands your personal situation. You should never act before seeking professional advice.

ISBN: 0-595-34496-8

Printed in the United States of America

Contents

1

Real Estate Investing as a Wealth Building Strategy

These are trying economic times. The job market is unsteady, people are concerned about their ability to save money for the future, and the stock market is always intimidating and unpredictable for the average investor. Many people are feeling vulnerable, and many are sinking into debt. Individuals and families who are struggling feel that they are a long way off from saving up the nest eggs that will pay for their kid's college or assure themselves a healthy retirement. First they have to pay off all that debt, and by the time they do that, they won't have the time to sock enough away for their future, they believe. So, they end up living for today with only vague hopes that "something" will happen in the future to reverse their situation. However "something" is unlikely to happen unless you make it happen. At the same time, many people are frustrated with the typical nine-to-five manner of making a living: long hours, short vacations, and they still don't earn enough to make ends meet. Families are realizing that the two wage earner model in this economic climate is not always family friendly. Families need more flexibility in their schedules and more time off to spend together.

More time off, more flexible schedules and more income…It sounds like an unrealistic wish list, doesn't it? However, these benefits are just what you can expect if you decide to make a career change and go into real estate. Unlike many other wealth building strategies, real estate investing has the power to remake people's financial lives in a bold and significant manner.

Real estate investing is not something that you should entertain as an option only for a future in which your financial situation has improved. Real estate investing is something you can start in the *near* future, regardless of your current situation. If you are in debt, you can't afford to wait until you are in the black again to begin investing. A real estate transaction that nets a sizeable profit may be just the strategy you need to address your debt problem. If you feel that your current income is too low to think about investing, then think again. Investing in an income property may add just the right amount of added monthly cash flow to get you back on track. Real estate is the one wealth building strategy in which everyone can get involved. Whether you are a college student, a job holder with a modest income, a stay at home mom, or even a retiree, you can make bold moves to improve your financial situation by investing in real estate today.

Take for example Mary and Paul, a young couple with whom I had the opportunity to speak not long ago. In their minds, their economic situation was dire. They felt they were deeply entrenched in credit card debt and that they didn't make enough from month to month even to think about saving money or paying down their debt. They felt continually "in the red" and were starting to feel fairly hopeless about the future. Like many other families of modest income right now, Mary and Paul do have a tight financial situation, no doubt about it, but they do have *something* that should allay their fears and make them feel more optimistic.

During our conversation, I reminded Mary and Paul of something that made them feel a lot better. You see, just a few years earlier they had invested in a home—a little white house in a nice neighborhood. It had required some fixing up, but Paul was handy, and he was able to take care of some repairs and upgrades without too much expense. Now they lived comfortably in that house while they worried about the state of their finances. They didn't seem to realize that while they perceived that they were sliding ever backwards each month, they were actually moving forward at the same time when they made their monthly mortgage payment each month. I encouraged them to sit down and do a few basic calculations regarding the down payment they had made on that house, the equity that they had paid into the house through their mortgage payments, and the appreciation on that house in the years that they had owned it. When they did, they discovered that their home equity actually exceeded, though not by a large margin, the amount of debt they owed. While they felt they were deep in debt, they were actually about even. Of course they could do better, but just knowing that they had a little something on their side helped to motivate them about their financial futures. The "little something" that could be on your side is real estate.

Of course Mary and Paul do not want to sell their house. Why should they give up the bedrock of their net worth? They are wise to let the power of appreciation work for them. Plus, they like their house and feel comfortable in it. However, if Mary and Paul really want to transform their financial situation, they would be wise to make the most of the investment they have and consider broadening the scope of their real estate investment. Those are the two skills I would like to teach you through this book. Whether you simply want to increase your wealth through wise homeownership, you want to invest in a few properties in order to supplement your income, or if you want to raise the roof on your dreams, this book can help you to get started.

Real estate can give *real* financial power to *real* people. It is the kind of wealth that doesn't evaporate out from under you. It is the resource that will always be desirable. When times get hard, people place even more value upon their property and their homes. Real estate investing, if done properly, is a sure way to build wealth. You know how much you will be making at your current job. Is it enough for you? You could open up your own business, but it is a risky endeavor and most businesses don't end up making money for the first couple of years. Can you afford that? For most of us, the answer is no. Real estate investing doesn't require a great deal of capital to start up, and your investing career can take a gradual course that doesn't put you at great financial risk, as business ownership might.

Real estate can protect you from excessive income taxes, and I am sure you have heard it referred to as a "shield against inflation." These are the kinds of protections that your wealth deserves. The big corporations have plenty of protections for their wealth, but it seems that middle and lower income citizens are always seeing their meager resources being depleted. Real Estate offers the common person a form of protection for their assets. Buying real estate is safe and profitable. Real estate is the most solid and tangible of all investments. Everyone needs shelter. Look around you, other investments are based in luxuries or commodities for which demand waxes and wanes. Real estate will always be in demand and the last hundred or so years of history has demonstrated how real estate offers steady appreciation over the long haul. Even during the Great Depression, real estate held its worth better than any other form of wealth. Real estate is an immensely democratic way to make money; nearly anyone can get involved at any time in their life's journey.

Take Karen for example. When she was in nursing school, she and her roommate moved into an adorable turn of the century Victorian home near the college, subdivided into three apartments. They really grew to appreciate their little apartment with its hardwood floors and its old fashioned charm. Karen and her roommate even made various improvements to the property—painting and minor repairs mostly. Well into her junior year, the landlord informed her he had decided to sell the place and that she would likely have to move when a new owner was found. Karen was devastated. However, after a talk with her parents, she had an idea. She decided to buy the place herself! While it was a novel action for a college student, Karen discovered that it was eminently possible to become a property owner while still in college. With a first time buyers loan program, and some help with the modest down payment from her parents, she was approved for the mortgage. During her senior year, she rented the two apartments to fellow college students and that income was almost sufficient to pay the mortgage. She made up the rest with the part time job she had always had anyway to help her pay her own rent. In this manner, she hobbled through the last year of college. When she graduated, she got a job that allowed her to quickly pay off the down payment money she had borrowed from her parents. Soon she was in a position to buy her own home, but she continued to rent out and maintain her first property, this time collecting rent on all three units that continued to pay the mortgage, but also gave her a small positive cash flow. By the time Karen married and moved into her third home, she had caught the real estate investing bug. She had seen how it had propelled her financial betterment through her early years as a professional. It was like fire under her rocket, and she continued to build momentum in her wealth building with a dual career as a nurse and a real estate investor. By the time she had her first child, his college fund was already well established, and you can bet that Karen and her husband will be in for a very comfortable retirement. It's all because Karen took that bold and unique step of investing in her first property while still in college.

What step do *you* need to take in order to control *your* financial destiny?

2

The Real Estate Self Inventory

When considering a move into the real estate business, the first thing you must do is to evaluate your needs and desires. There are a multitude of different ways to invest in real estate. How you do it will depend upon your financial needs, your professional aspirations, your personality, and your lifestyle. It may be that you just want to start out your financial life with the solid investment of home ownership. Many homeowners don't consider themselves real estate investors and think of their home only as the place they live. However, homeownership can be a powerful centerpiece of your overall wealth-building plan if you approach the purchase, maintenance, and the monthly investment into a home as a real estate investor would. This book will help you do that.

It might be that you already have a career that you really enjoy and that career takes up a good deal of your time. However, you would like to enhance your income and progress more quickly toward your long-term financial goals. In this case, part time real estate investing might be just the answer for you. Perhaps you could start with a small, single-family rental property and go from there, adding properties as you go and as you encounter good deals.

It might be, however, that you are disenchanted with the "rat race" and are looking for a way to seize control of your destiny. Maybe you covet the freedom of being self employed, making your own hours, and making just as much money as you like, free from bosses who have the power to decide whether or not you deserve a raise in pay. Maybe you are a stay at home mother and you don't like the idea of returning to work, sending your kids to an after school program, and not being able to easily extricate yourself from work when your kids are sick or on vacation. Mothers need freedom and flexibility, but in this economy, they also need substantial incomes. Real estate can provide both.

Of course, many real estate success stories are a combination of different forms of investing. A typical scenario might involve a person who starts out as a homeowner, gains an interest in and a respect for the power of real estate, and then starts dabbling part time. Perhaps they bought a new house, but held on to the old, or they bought a rental property. Or perhaps they spotted a good deal, fixed it up and sold it. For some time, such a real estate investor might do real estate part time while still maintaining a full time job. But then they start to notice how their real estate income is starting to dwarf their regular paycheck. They start to feel itchy and agitated at work, thinking about how they are spending eight hours a day earning a modest wage when they could be out making their real estate investment holdings grow. So, at some point, many of these part time real estate investors decide to take the leap and make real estate their full time occupation. It is at this juncture that the limits are truly unleashed on people's dreams. If they could do so well doing real estate part time, imagine what they could do when they begin to devote themselves fully to the task? In such a way, many a real estate millionaire is born.

Real estate is one of those things that you have to take step-by-step, deal-by-deal. It requires patience and diligence and a willingness to educate yourself every step of the way. This book is a great starting place.

Now, you may like the idea of being self-employed and making a great deal more money than you are now. However, if you decide to devote yourself to being a real estate investor, you have to decide if you like the lifestyle and world of the typical real estate investor. After all, despite the freedom and potential for a passive wealth stream, real estate investing is a job that requires commitment and hard work. The demands of this job may not be for you, especially on a full time basis.

Some people are better suited for the cozy confines of the office, a well-defined scope of responsibility, the support of a network of colleagues, and the security of a regular paycheck. Let's take a look at the typical day of a real estate investor, and you can begin to imagine if such a life is for you.

Meet Steve. He is a full time real estate investor with a lively and diversified real estate portfolio. He buys and maintains rental properties, has a couple of commercial properties, and he also enjoys purchasing single family homes at a real bargain, fixing them up and selling them for a profit. Succinctly put, Steve is always on the lookout for a real estate bargain, and he sizes up each property in terms of how it can best serve his wealth-building journey. On a typical day, Steve might wake up a bit tired. It is not unusual for him to have received one or more calls in the middle of the night from a tenant. In this case of this morning, Steve was up at 4:00 am, on the phone, dealing with a neighbor dispute in one of his apartment buildings. It seems that an argument turned into a broken window in the early morning hours, and the police were called. He places dealing with that situation high on his to-do list for the day. Over breakfast, Steve carefully scrutinizes the real estate sections of two local papers. He also scans the paper for pertinent community news: divorces, foreclosures, crime reports and even the obituaries. Steve is a news hound with a close ear to the ground of this community. He needs to know about local economic trends and just about everything that influences the way people live in his community. As he reads, he circles an advertisement for an interesting property and takes note of a promising foreclosure.

As Steve heads over to deal with the scene at the apartment building, he decides to drive through the neighborhood in which the foreclosed property was listed. As he drives, he carefully evaluates the neighborhood. He cranes his neck at every "For Sale" sign, looks at the paint jobs on the houses, the landscaping, what kind of cars are in the driveways. He is always looking for signs. Is this neighborhood in decline or does it represent a mixed economy? Does it seem poised to experience an upswing? He stops the car periodically to scribble something in his notebook. (Real estate investors tend to be slow drivers.) He sees a "For Sale by Owner" sign and stops the car to take a closer look. He hops out of the car when he sees the owner raking in the backyard. The two chat for a good fifteen minutes. Steve asks about the house, but also subtly probes for information about the neighborhood and even the foreclosed house down the way. He gets the backstory. When he hops back into his car, having made an appointment to tour the property later on, he quickly heads to the address of the foreclosed property he had read about in the paper. He notices the signs of disrepair on the outside and calculates in his head how much it might cost to repair the vinyl siding and tear out the old dilapidated pool in back. He peeks in windows and kicks his way through the overgrown weeds, scaring a couple of stray cats in the bargain. Good thing he didn't wear an expensive Italian suit to work…

Realizing it is growing late, Steve gets back in his car and heads across town to the apartment property that had robbed him of sleep the night before—a medium sized building with eight rental units. There have been problems there before. When he arrives, he talks to the tenant whose window has been broken. He calls up his handyman to have him fix the window quickly. In the mean time, he helps the tenant to secure the window with a board he finds in the maintenance shed. He then goes knocking on the door of the apartment in which the other party in the dispute is said to live. An older woman answers the door and repeats what she has already told the police: she thinks her nephew may have broken the window. He doesn't live in the building, and she doesn't know where he is. Steve will have to take a look at the police report and deal with his insurance company later. While he is at the apartment building, various tenants file out to talk to him. Unit 8 has a broken faucet. Steve gets on his cell to his handyman to add this repair to his duty list. A man from Unit 5 says that he saw the altercation and contends that it wasn't the woman's nephew; it was her son. Steve listens, but feels resigned to letting the police sort it all out. Someone else talks to him about getting an extension on her rent and Steve agrees, but insists that the $15 late fee will still apply.

By the time Steve pulls out of the apartment parking lot, it is lunchtime. He decides to head over to have lunch at a diner in a neighborhood he has been keeping his eye on. There is an old office complex there that has been vacant for months. He figures the owners must be getting pretty desperate. Still, he thinks the purchase might be risky if the neighborhood is in decline. At the restaurant, he looks out the window, taking note of new businesses, the kinds of cars that are parked there, the way the people are dressed, and other signs. He also talks to a few of the restaurant patrons, asking them idle questions about the area and chatting in general.

After lunch, Steve heads over to his accountant's office. He's gotten excited about the office building and wants his accountant to go ahead and run a little financial analysis on the property. While he is sitting in the office, waiting, his cell phone rings. It's his contractor. He needs to go over and inspect an apartment complex he has been rehabbing. The contractor seems to think the interior is finished. After chatting with his accountant for a good half hour, Steve heads over to tour the apartment complex. He needs to assess whether or not it is ready to be put on the market. Steve finds that, unfortunately, it is not. The new hardware on the sinks has caused some damage to the porcelain. His blood pressure momentarily rises as he talks to the contractor. Will they now have to replace the sinks? The contractor thinks not; there is a product on the market that can patch porcelain and then they can repaint. Steve calms down and answers his cell phone. It is his handyman. The window is done but he can't find the tenant for whom the faucet needed to be replaced....

And on to home and dinner...Steve could work all night, but he chooses not to. His cell phone will ring, but the rest of the business can be put off until the next day. He goes to bed tired but energized with visions of the new office complex he is planning to buy and to transform into the centerpiece of a rising neighborhood.

Ok. So ask yourself. Does Steve's day excite you or horrify you? Knowing that you can make your real estate investing lifestyle your own, there are some features of the lifestyle that are fairly typical. First of all, you may have noticed that Steve had a great deal of mobility and variety in his day. He was in his car a lot. He had to be open to being called hither and thither to respond to issues with his properties or to jump on developing real estate prospects. Do you feel constrained in an office doing one thing all day long? If so, the mobile nature of real estate investing might be attractive to you.

Another feature of Steve's day is that he is called upon to do a good deal of detective work. He has to be constantly on the lookout for signs of a good real estate deal. A good real estate investor is someone who is enthusiastically attuned to details, who likes to drive around sizing up neighborhoods and properties, combing through the paper and talking to people. If you are a curious person who enjoys the thrill of investigative probing, real estate investing may be something you will really enjoy.

Another aspect of Steve's day that is probably a must for every real estate investor is that Steve has a lot of interaction with people. He has to be willing to jump out of his car and strike up a conversation with a seller who happens to be outside. He receives a lot of valuable information through good old fashioned, friendly chatting. He also has to deal with a lot of cell phone calls and quite a few tenant issues, not all of them pleasant. If dealing with people makes you curl up inside with anxiety, then a career as a full time real estate investor may not be for you. An outgoing, assertive personality is probably best for such a career. Many real estate investors, however, find that they do not like dealing with tenant issues and go on to hire a management company to do that for them. (More on those later.) However, even with a management company in place, a wise landlord will keep close tabs on his or her property.

Steve's lifestyle is far from glamorous. If you can't stand poking your nose into the fragrant air of a foreclosed building or if chatting with patrons at a diner would seem awkward to you, then you may want to rethink your career path. A real estate agent needs to blend in with the community; to really be a part of it. Most real estate investors drive economy cars and don't wear designer clothes and high heeled shoes. A bargain property is often a dirty, sometimes even smelly one! Despite the scarcity of, many real estate investors really enjoy "being out there," maintaining an active interest in their community, and having contact with a variety of people. While they miss out on driving a Jag and dining only in the most expensive restaurants, they make up for that by seeing the balances in their financial portfolios consistently on the rise. And of course, if freedom is your muse, then I can't imagine a better livelihood for you. Another thing that drives people into careers in real estate is a genuine love of homes. Some people routinely scour the MLS listings on the Internet, even when they aren't in the market for a house. They crane their necks at every "For Sale" sign on their way to work, and they love to go to those "Open Houses" just out of sheer curiosity. They know the different between a Cape and a Craftsman and are avid viewers of all those home and garden programs on cable television today. A good real estate investor may simply really enjoy real estate. If you are handy with tools and have a good decorator's eye, that can't hurt either.

You may have noticed that the stereotypical persona of the real estate agent is male. You know, the assertive, handy with a hammer, hard-boiled detective, driving with one hand, cigar in the other stereotype? Well I'm here to tell you that women all over this country are remaking this image. In many ways the life of a real estate agent is uniquely suited to women. After all, many women are looking for careers that offer them the flexibility of being there for their families with the benefit of decisive income potential. Women tend to be fairly community minded and often enjoy chatting on their daily walks through the neighborhood. They often have their "ear to the ground;" they may know who is getting divorced, which house on the block has had a fire in the past, and why the Feingold's down the street are *really* moving. While tenant problems can be intimidating for anyone, especially women, there are those women whose maternal personas work wonders on the ruffled feathers of their tenants. On the other hand, many women are intimidated by the financial aspect of the profession. Their upbringings may have shielded them from an intimate knowledge of equity and leverage and all of the necessary calculations inscribed in the real estate investing books. Don't let this stop you. There will be an accountant at your side, and you do have the capacity to learn the money business. Real estate is a great teacher. It allows you to practice what you learn each step of the way and learn at your own pace. It is my sincere belief that women have a great deal to contribute to the landscape of real estate investing.

So, perhaps you have now gained as sense of what is involved in being a real estate investor. You probably already can sense whether you want to enter the game at the level of homeownership, part time, or full time real estate investing. The point is that you are beginning to see how real estate can be a powerful source of fuel for your journey toward economic security. The way that you approach real estate will have something to do with your economic reality and your economic dreams.

Of course, if you are currently a renter with a modest income, your first step will probably be buying your own home. (Many first time homeowners, however, have had good luck with buying a multi-family property like a duplex and using the rental income to help with their mortgage.) Regardless of where you are, however, before you start making real estate investment decisions, you have to determine the best mode for accumulating money for your particular situation. In real estate, you can make money three ways:

Future income

A sizable, quick profit

A steady, monthly cash flow

Ideally, you can make money in all three ways, but in starting out you have to make some decisions. If you are saving for the future, for your kid's education or for your retirement, you are wise to hold onto a property and let time do its magic. The property will appreciate in value over the years and you will make a large profit on it at some future date. This is the manner in which homeownership is a wealth-building move, but this can also be the case with a rental property held over a period of time as long as it stands up to the wear and tear of tenant occupancy. This is the "nest egg" approach and it works via the fairly reliable forces of appreciation. In real estate, time is on your side.

Perhaps, though, you need money more immediately than that. Maybe you need money to pay off a large debt, or you want to raise a pool of money to use to fund a new investment. This can be accomplished by purchasing properties at a bargain price, doing smart rehabilitation, and then quickly re-selling the property at a profit.

Finally, you may find yourself in need of an income boost. You want a steady, monthly cash flow that will keep you out of debt, enable you to reinvest, and nourish your entire financial picture over the long haul. In such a case you are wise to buy one or more income generating rental properties. They will provide you with a monthly income to pay the mortgage and give you a steady positive cash flow that will allow you to hold onto the property and enjoy maximum appreciation value in the future.

There are advantages and disadvantages to each of these modes of wealth building through real estate that will be discussed throughout this book. Most full time real estate investors diversify themselves amongst all three. That is how the wealth *really* starts to flow your way. The nice thing about real estate, however, is how investment strategies can be tailored to work with any situation in which you may find yourself.

3

The First Step: Homeownership

Let me first clear up a misconception. If you own your own home, you *are* a real estate investor. If you approach the purchase with the level of seriousness that you would if you did real estate investing for a living, then you will realize maximum return on your investment. Many people don't sufficiently realize the investment potential of their home because they make the purchase with the levity and impulsiveness that one might display when picking out a new car or even a dress, but buying a house is different than these other purchases, because a house isn't a material good to be used and eventually discarded when it depreciates in value or simply falls apart. Your house is an investment, and its value should grow substantially if you make the right purchasing decision and handle homeownership in a wise manner. The good news is that in the purchase of your new home, you will learn the basics of real estate investing and you will be poised to take the next step if you choose to do so. Many real estate investors get the fever for real estate investing during the purchase of their first home. They find themselves enjoying the process of viewing properties, and they get a sense of the deals that are out there. They simply don't want to stop after they close the deal on their own home.

Is homeownership for you? Most likely, it is. Why pay rent when you could be paying into a solid investment that could be a springboard for future wealth? It doesn't make much sense. Buying your own home is one of the smartest initial wealth building moves you can make. Wouldn't you rather make a monthly investment in your own property rather than in your landlords? In most cases, it makes a great deal more sense to invest in your own property than to pay rent. Many people don't realize that they can actually afford to buy a home, but the vast majority of people can, especially today. I know one young couple, Eric and Mya, who recently returned back to their hometown to live near family after Mya suffered an injury that forced her to drop out of school. This could have been a devastating blow to a young couple just starting out their lives. Here they were, nearly penniless, already derailed from their career paths. Well, Eric and Mya are not your average young couple. They are filled with optimism and a can-do attitude. When they returned home, Eric landed a fairly low paying job for a social service agency, and Mya, while recovering from her injury, found a job that allowed her to work about ten hours a week, bringing in a fairly negligible income. At this point, this couple could hardly afford rent, and rather than imposing upon family members, they ended up camping out much of the summer. But, when the end of September rolled around and the leaves began to change colors…Eric and Mya were homeowners!

How did they do it? Well, they were determined, optimistic, and they did their homework. They found a property that was available through foreclosure. They educated themselves about first time homeowner programs for people with low incomes. They made use of a local grant program for rehabbing properties that helped them get the property into habitable condition. Now each month as they pay their mortgage, they are setting themselves up for a much brighter future. As Mya's injury resolves itself and both of their professional lives develop, they will be on solid ground as the leap of homeownership is already behind them. If they could do it, with all of their obstacles, *you can too.*

If you have already bought a home, then you probably learned a great deal about real estate investing in the process. Or perhaps you made a hasty decision without educating yourself first and now you are living with some measure of regret. However, it is never too late to learn the fundamentals, and in the world of real estate investing, the first building block is the purchase of the single family home.

Many people believe that they don't have enough savings or a high enough income to own their own home. Eric and Mya's experience demonstrates, however, that nearly anyone can become a homeowner. Often your mortgage payments will not be significantly higher than your rent payments were. (Your landlord is probably trying to charge you the amount that will enable him to pay his mortgage on the place, perhaps with a little extra for positive cash flow.) The good news about our current economy is that banks and lending institutions are motivated to get people into homes. There are programs out there that can get you into a home with a very low down payment. Research has demonstrated to lenders that people who have paid lower down payments are not significantly more likely to default on their debt and face foreclosure, so it is now in the best interest of lenders to make homeownership possible for a wider group of people.

Is home ownership always advisable? Usually, yes, and even more so for people with modest incomes. Homeownership is the best way to start saving for the future. However, there are some situations in which one might want to explore other options or delay homeownership:

#1: You don't plan to be in the same place for very long. It usually takes three to five years for a purchased home to realize the benefits of appreciation. You don't want to be paying the fees and costs associated with buying a house if you aren't going to realize a sufficient return on your investment through appreciation. So, if you aren't thrilled with your current location or if your job may require you to relocate, you may want to delay home ownership. I do know several real estate investors who bought a home during their younger, unsettled years, and then had to relocate shortly after. Instead of selling their newly acquired home, however, they held onto the property and managed it from a distance. In such a way they were able to pay the extra mortgage and benefit from the forces of appreciation. Many of us would have difficulty affording the transaction costs associated with the purchase of one home without selling the former one, however, and management

from a distance can be tricky. Usually it is advisable to be somewhat settled before you invest in a home.

#2: *You don't have the funds or the time to property maintain your home.* You don't want to purchase a property and then let it go to seed. You must be able to budget for occasional repairs and be willing to hire labor or do-it-yourself when it comes to routine maintenance like landscaping, cleaning gutters, chimney maintenance, resealing your deck, and so on. Don't let yourself be deterred by this reality of home ownership, however. The financial and personal investments you make in your home will come back to you because they are investments in an appreciable asset. (If the cost and labor of maintenance and upkeep seems prohibitive to you, don't let your home buying dreams die; consider buying a condominium. With a condominium, the property is shared and you will have at least one wall in common with another owner. You may also have some restrictions regarding modifications and lifestyle. For instance, you may have to keep your noise level down after hours and may not be able to barbeque on your balcony. However, there are some significant advantages as well. For a monthly fee, all the maintenance and upkeep on the outside of your property will be taken care of for you. You might enjoy significantly more elaborately landscaped grounds than you could have provided yourself as a homeowner. You may even have access to a pool, a playground and/or a fitness facility. You will not need to spend time cleaning gutters, mowing lawns or painting fences. People who are very busy and not very "handy" might find a condominium to be the perfect solution. Condominiums are often best for people without children and for singles—the opportunities for socialization are great.) The bottom line is, don't be naÔve about the maintenance and upkeep requirements of being a homeowner.

#3: *You live in a city and the housing prices are out of this world.* Home ownership for people in cities can be particularly difficult. Many city apartment dwellers don't even entertain the possibility of home ownership. If this is your situation, you have several options:

Investigate special buyers programs: You aren't the only one who is experiencing the high cost of urban property. People can't afford to purchase the buildings in which they live, and so high rollers from other communities purchase them, rent them out, often turn them into slums—you know the story. This is a social problem, and where there is a social problem there are special programs. Your city may have an urban renewal agenda that will help you to purchase a home or even the apartment building that you currently occupy. City planners know that when a building is owned by someone who is a member of the community, that building is less likely to be turned into a dilapidated slum. Don't simply assume that you can't be a property owner just because you live in a city.

Buy into a co-op. Co-ops are multi-family properties (usually apartment buildings) that differ from condominiums in that when you purchase a co-op, you are not buying an individual unit within the building. Instead you are buying shares in a corporation and that gives you the right to occupy one of the units. You become a shareholder and help to set and live by certain community rules. You pay a monthly maintenance fee and thus such things are taken care of for you. Co-ops can be a good investment as the prosperity of the entire piece of property, often in hot urban markets, is shared. However, it is also risky in that if one shareholder defaults on his or her responsibilities, the other shareholders absorb the loss. This is why obtaining a co-op mortgage is a paperwork nightmare, and expect to be scrutinized down to the cellular level. Co-ops tend to be for people of higher incomes with good credit records.

Move to the suburbs. This won't solve the problem of urban flight, buy you aren't in charge of solving major social problems. While I encourage you to consider city property, you have the right to be a homeowner and if it takes moving to the suburbs, that is a solid option for you. Perhaps you'll like it there.

Financing the First Home

When I was just out of college in the early 1990's, my friends and I were under the impression that obtaining a home mortgage would be extremely unlikely for us. We tended to be a little disillusioned about our ability to really "make it" in the economy as it was, and so we tended to live for the day and try not to think about the future. As a result, a lot of us ran up a good deal of debt and didn't do much saving. While perhaps a little bit overly pessimistic, we weren't half wrong about how out of reach buying a home was for us at the time. At that time, in order to even think about applying for a mortgage, you had to have a solid income, a spotless credit record, and a 20% down payment. No wonder we tried to define our lives outside of the picket fence ideal. Very few individuals first starting out can confidently walk into the bank with all of those variables in their favor.

However, things have changed since that difficult economic period. The banking industry, recognizing the lost financial opportunities that result when an entire generation seems to give up hope in the American Dream, has worked with politicians to make homeownership a realistic goal for first time buyers a top priority. First time homeownership programs like Fannie Mae (the Federal National Mortgage Association) have motivated banks around the country to open up their lending practices by promising to buy mortgages for which the borrowers have put down as little as 3 or 5%. Many people who do not consider themselves eligible for homeownership are stunned to find out that they now stand a good chance of being able to finance a home. I know people with terrible credit, even bankruptcies, who are now homeowners. They aren't paying the lowest interest rates, but they have their home and they can work to rebuild their financial good name through scrupulous repayment of their mortgage.

No matter what your financial situation, it doesn't hurt to get some information about what it will take to get you into your first home. Your local bank will be happy to consult with you about homeownership, free of charge. Just call to make an appointment. You don't have to be ready to make a home purchase to visit with a bank or mortgage lender. It is wise to do some preliminary comparison-shopping. You can also learn a great deal and do a myriad of financial computations online. However, I often find it is best to talk to someone with a pulse who can answer your questions and lead you through the process in a way that you can really understand it. You may want to start with the bank with whom you do the rest of your financial business. You are their customer, and they should be eager to treat you well to protect their other investments in you. (If they don't treat you well, exercise your option to go somewhere else.) When you go, bring in your bank statements and a copy of your pay stubs. If you don't have an idea of how much debt you owe, then write down all of your outstanding debt and your monthly payments before you go. Regardless, just do it, and don't be intimidated. It is your right to own a home, and you should be pursuing this goal. Don't delay this step!

Your bank should be able to quickly answer two important preliminary questions:

> Your approval price (the maximum amount you can spend on a house).

> The approximate amount to money you will need for down payment and closing.

The amount of the mortgage for which you qualify is primarily based upon two things: your income and the minimum monthly payments you already owe toward debt. The bank not only wants to make sure that you have sufficient income to make monthly payments, but also that you don't currently have so much debt that you will become overextended if you have a mortgage.

Once you get the approval price, you must ask yourself whether or not you can buy a home that will be appropriate for your family in that price range. At this point you may want to look around at some houses to see what different increments of money will buy. What does a $120,000 house look like in your area? How about a $150,000 one? House prices vary widely depending upon location. A luxury home price in one area might buy little more than a shack in another. In some areas, you can buy a very nice home in the $80,000 or even below range. You need to get a sense of your local market. Don't make the mistake of thinking that because you qualify for a certain amount, you should pay that amount. You may be able to qualify for far more than you can actually afford on a month-to-month basis. However, you need to first assess whether or not you qualify for the kind of house you need. If you find that your approval price is too low, one way to raise it is to reduce your monthly debt. If you, for example, got rid of a $200 a month car payment, that is another $200 that the bank figures you can spend on a mortgage payment and your approval price will go up.

If you can't trim your monthly debt, or if that is not a significant factor, then you will be surprised just how much a small hike in your monthly income can make a difference. If you have only one income, can the other spouse or partner take on a part time job? Maybe it is time to ask for a raise. As a loyal employee, you should make a sufficient income to provide adequate shelter for yourself and your family. Respectfully walk into your bosses' office and discuss the matter with him or her. Emphasize the value that you bring to the business, your length of service, the quality of your work, your excellent work habits, and so forth. Your boss may admire your forthrightness. Explain that your current salary is inadequate to allow you to qualify for a mortgage on a suitable home. If he is wise, your boss will recognize that this is not just *your* problem. If his employees are not making living wages, he will soon have a turnover problem. Solvent employees, settled in their own homes, are more reliable and loyal, and they stay longer. Even a small raise in pay may make the difference in your approval price. If your request for a small raise is rejected, this may be an indication that you need to find a better job.

Get a real sense of the cost of owning a home:

When you go through the real estate listings online, you may feel a surge of encouragement when they list the anticipated monthly mortgage prices for various properties. "Only $660 dollars a month? I can afford that!" Remember, they are trying to sell you a house. Your monthly cost will be significantly higher than that—probably close to double the number tempting you on the screen. Be aware that your monthly bill will be comprised of more than just the mortgage principle. You will also be bundling the following into your monthly payment: homeowner's insurance, prime mortgage insurance, property taxes, and if you are in a flood zone, flood insurance. Your lender will calculate all of these in order to come up with a realistic estimate of your monthly payment, or monthly housing costs.

What your lender may not discuss with you is the other costs of owning a home that you must take into account. Each year you will have a range of expenses associated with owning your home. These will vary from year to year. One year you will have to buy a snow blower, replace the water heater, and resurface the driveway. Another year you may have to replace a roof. As you look at various houses, keep in mind maintenance and upkeep costs. You can keep these costs down by buying a house with lots of updates and renovations, but of course the cost of such a house will probably be higher. A smaller yard will have smaller upkeep requirements. A pool is an attractive feature, but it can be expensive to maintain. Keep these issues in mind so that you are not taken by surprise by such expenses. If your income will be budgeted down to the cent and if you have no cushion fund, then you will frequently be derailed by various "emergencies" that really are the routine expectations of home ownership. In fact, it would be wise to budget a certain amount monthly to account for maintenance, upkeep and replacement costs associated with owning your home. If that means that you should buy a $120,000 house rather than the $150,000 house for which you qualify, then so be it.

When you go to the bank to fact find, chances are the mortgage broker will give you a list of documents that you will need in order to apply for a mortgage. The documents required, and how far back they must go, will vary depending upon the institution, but they will probably include:

> Check stubs over a certain period (probably 3 months)
>
> Bank statements
>
> Tax Returns
>
> Statements for all open credit accounts
>
> Various identification documents

If the broker doesn't give you a list of required documents, request one. Gathering the necessary materials to apply for a mortgage can be very time consuming, and it can delay your application process. You need to get started once a day. Good record keepers might have all of the necessary materials on hand, neatly filed away, but the rest of us may need to make some phone calls. The paperwork was the most intimidating part of buying a first home for me. I am quite a disorganized person, and at that point in my life, I never saved *anything*. That list of required documents, now grubby with coffee stains, ruled my life for several weeks. I had to start from scratch. Each day I focused on one item on the list. One day I called to order a couple of past tax returns. (And yes, I was on the phone for a couple of hours.) Another day I called human resources at my husband and I's employer and requested past check stubs. One by one I called our creditors to request statements. Yes, I spent quite a bit of time on the phone. Yes, I paid quite a bit in copy request fees. Yes, I faced the snippy attitude of a good number of administrative personnel. Then I had to wait to receive all these documents in the mail. But by God, I did it! When I had that folder stuffed with my completed application materials my pride knew no bounds. I really felt it was my first truly grown up moment, and it was certainly one of those personal growth experiences. Hopefully you are more organized than I, but it goes to show there is hope for everyone.

Raising Down payment and Closing Costs

The first time is the hardest time in terms of purchasing real estate. Your payment history is unproven and you don't have one property to leverage in order to buy another one. However, the important thing is turn intangible fear into tangible information. Find out how much you will have to pay up front to get into your first home and then go about methodically accumulating that amount of money. While down payments used to be prohibitively large, it is now possible to get a down payment amount of 3% of the value of the house through programs like Fannie Mae. That means that if you were buying a house for which the asking price was $100,000 you would only need $3,000 as a down payment. You may also need money for closing costs and lawyer's fees, but it is sometimes possible to finance these charges. Let's take a conservative approach and imagine that you will need $5,000. Not all of us have $3,000, much less $5,000 extra sitting in our bank accounts. However, amassing this much money is a manageable goal for most of us. Use the following strategies, or a combination of them:

Start Saving! Open a savings account specifically for your down payment and closing costs funds. That way, your extra money won't get swallowed up in routine or impulse expenditures. Vow not to touch this money until you are closing on your new house. Keep a vivid image of that moment in your head as motivation. Determine the amount needed, establish a timeline, and then start a savings plan to get you there in that timeframe. Since the goal of homeownership is so important, both financially and emotionally, you may want to institute some temporary, really sacrificial savings measures to meet your goal. I know people who didn't eat out for a year in the name of homeownership. Brown bag it at lunch time. Stop getting your hair professionally done. Cancel your cable. You can always reinstitute your luxurious lifestyle when you are happily ensconced in your new home, and having done without, your old lifestyle will seem doubly decadent and enjoyable. Make it a game and keep your eye on the prize.

Supplement your income. In order to feed your new savings account, consider additional part time or freelance work. I know one young woman who took on a weekend job as a waitress in a nightclub in addition to her nine to five weekday job as an insurance claims adjustor. She was pretty exhausted with this schedule, of course, but felt motivated and energized as her savings grew and her dream of homeownership was becoming more realistic every day. She made sure that 100% of her new part time income went into her savings account. She kept up that schedule for ten grueling months, but now she is a homeowner, and working just one job seems like a pretty light load in comparison to her year and a half of sacrificing for her future.

Sell a Luxury Item. Home ownership requires you to alter your priorities. You might want to consider parting with a big-ticket item in order to make this satisfying goal a reality. Are you spending hundreds each month on payments toward your prestige vehicle? Imagine the prestige of throwing parties your very own living room! You can sell that car, dump the monthly payments and pay cash for a used car with good gas mileage. If you continue to pay out your previous car payment, but instead put it in your savings account, before long you will be a homeowner, and you will still get to work in the morning. Is that piece of jewelry sitting in a box on your dresser more important than your right to sit on your back porch and watch the sun go down every evening? Few things are that precious.

Borrow. Financial experts generally warn against borrowing money except for the acquisition of an asset with significant powers of appreciation. Real estate is such an asset. Lenders will look at the amount of down payment that comes out of your own money as a sign of your financial solvency, but as studies show that such factors are not reliable indictors of who will face foreclosure and who will not, more and more are willing to consider money that is loaned to you. You can consider borrowing from an insurance policy or a 401K or borrowing or accepting a gift from a family member as a way to raise money. If you do borrow from another investment, try to pay it back as soon as possible. Your loan of $1,000 could end up costing you several times that in the life of your investment.

<u>Save unexpected income</u>. Do you get an annual bonus or an extra paycheck during the holidays? Perhaps you unexpectedly inherit some money or receive a healthy tax return. Generally, we tend to throw this money to the wind and months later all traces of it are gone. Instead, leverage any unexpected income into more wealth by placing it in a savings account to be used for a real estate transaction.

A combination of several of these strategies may just do the trick. For example, my husband and I, to raise down payment and closing costs on our first home, saved a portion of the money over a year's time, accepted a family gift, and borrowed from a 401K.

The point? Raising the lump sum you need to buy a home is something that you really *can do*. It just takes a little effort, sacrifice and forethought. After you have made your first home purchase, you can periodically use these savings strategies when raising the capital for your early real estate ventures.

Maximizing the return on home ownership.

Allow yourself time to build equity

Generally speaking, unless it is a real fixer, sells at an unbelievable price, and you do rapid remodeling and then turn it over for much more than you bought it, a home's investment potential is not realized for several years. A home becomes an asset if given enough *time*. The

cost of buying a home—the down payments, closing costs and reloca-
tion expenses—will eat up the profits you would normally make off a
home purchase in a shorter timeframe. The longer you hold onto your
home, the more equity you build because over time a higher percentage
of your monthly payment goes toward paying the mortgage principle.
The nice thing about buying a house is that paying your mortgage payment each month is money well spent. Each month it is an investment.
And the more you pay, the higher your return will be.

Consider mortgage repayment acceleration

Many homebuyers sit in their lender's office, holding their breath, *hoping* for the lowest possible monthly payment on their home purchase.
Such a hope might be realistic in light of your income and expenses,
but it is a bit like hoping for a punch in the stomach. A low monthly
payment can end up costing you thousands of dollars over the course
of your mortgage. Making a higher mortgage payment is not a penalty;
it is actually a privilege. It saves you money in interest payments and
shortens the length of time you are making payments. When you own
your home, free and clear, imagine what you could do with the money
you have been sending each month for your mortgage payments. That
will go a long way toward helping you to enjoy a worry free retirement.

Realizing the benefits of an accelerated mortgage repayment plan
does not have to mean a dramatic change in your lifestyle, or years of
self-sacrifice. Just one extra mortgage payment per year can shave years
off of the length of your mortgage, and you build home equity with
each extra dollar you invest. An extra $100 per month toward your
mortgage can make a striking difference as well. If you are able to free
up money in one area through smart savings strategies, you can divert
it toward your mortgage and you will never miss it. For many of us, as
first time homeowners, even an extra $50 or so dollars per month
toward our mortgages would be difficult to accomplish. If that is the
case, don't worry. You are doing great work investing each month in a

powerful source of equity. In the future you will have added income or an unexpected financial windfall to put toward your mortgage.

Maintain and improve your property.

With home ownership, little problems can become big problems very quickly. If you don't take care of that water leak for $250 in materials and labor, then you could be facing a problem with mold and water damage that could cost thousands and make your home very difficult to sell. Branches that don't get trimmed back away from your house can result in your needing a new roof a couple of years down the line. Routine maintenance saves you money and protects your investment.

Similarly, improvements to your home also are investment that will really pay off. So, rather than blow a bunch of money this year on a vacation to the islands, why not put in an extra bathroom or give your kitchen a facelift? These kinds of improvements can greatly enhance the resale value on your home and you will enjoy them as well. Keep on investing in your home and your payoff will increase.

4

Real Estate Investing Style and Strategies

It may be that you have a career you enjoy, a good retirement plan, and you have plotted your life's financial course to enjoy a safe and comfortable future. That is a feat worthy of congratulations. But maybe you don't want to stop there. Maybe you want to work your financial know-how toward accelerated wealth building, so that you go beyond security and into abundance. Among the options for such an endeavor, real estate is one of the soundest options.

Whether you want to own a handful of properties as part of your overall portfolio, or you decide that real estate is in your blood and that you want to devote yourself full time to buying, renovating, selling, managing properties, any life change requires that you do a lot of thinking, gain the necessary information and come up with a game plan.

With real estate, knowledge is key. You need to know properties. You need to know areas. You need to know markets. You need to know about smart negotiation, property management, and the way property appreciates. The good news is that, if you did it right, you have already learned a great deal about real estate when you bought your own home.

As a real estate investor you have a variety of kind of real estate to consider:

Single Family Houses

Apartments

Office Buildings

Shopping Centers

Land

Other: Industrial properties, warehouses, hotels, etc.

Most experts recommend that the beginning real estate investor concentrate on single-family homes, multi-family homes, and small apartment buildings. Office buildings are a little more risky than homes or apartments, because no matter what the economy, people still need places to live while businesses can go away and not be replaced by new ones. Whole business districts can dry up, never to return. (Still, they can also be very profitable. In dynamic business areas, rent can run very high.)

The two most important warnings for the beginning real estate investor to heed are:

Start gradually: Start by buying one piece of property, fixing it up and perhaps renting it out. Learn all you can about the process. Then turn your attention toward another type of property. This way you are minimizing your risk and learning what you need to know along the way.

Maintain an adequate cash flow. Remember that buying the property is not the only expense. A real estate investment is not a good one if you cannot afford to protect your asset. You will need to have money to pay for routine maintenance and unexpected damage or repairs. Otherwise, you will have bought a property only to become a slumlord. And you certainly don't want to do that. The smart real estate investor vows to bring to an end the era of tenant exploitation and mistreatment and will demonstrate to other investors that social and financial goals can go hand in hand. You want to attract a tenant whom you respect and whom respects your property as well. Your job will be a great deal easier if you have happy, long-term tenants and a well maintained property. Plus, when you maintain your property, you increase the property values of the neighborhood, which greatly enhances the value of your investment. Do not buy more properties until you have created the cash flow necessary to maintain the one you have.

Investing Styles

The beauty of real estate is that it is a career that can be customized to fit nearly any goal, personality or lifestyle. It all depends upon what you enjoy about working in real estate and what your goals are.

For instance, one of my favorite stories involves a group of former stay at home mom's who went into real estate together. They all share a love of finding homes with a great deal of potential and then fixing them up and renting them out. What they really enjoy is buying the property and then all putting on their overalls, going over together and quickly cleaning, painting, planting flowers and other light rehab projects. They turn on music, chatter, and bond, really enjoying the process. Their interest in rehabilitation is one of the primary reasons they went into real estate. They also don't mind the work associated with renting properties. There are a good number of them in the group, so no one person gets overwhelmed with tenant calls or "land-lady" responsibilities. As mothers with an active interest in the community, they take pride in being hands-on, responsible property owners and take seriously their responsibility to provide safe, affordable housing to renters. As they buy more and more properties to rent, they are really making a difference in the quality of their community. They like that.

Other real estate investor's however, are more fascinated with the negotiation process, the structure of a deal, and creative modes of financing. They don't want to be spending time in their overalls or mediating tenant disputes. They want to be out making more deals. These types of investors tend to favor quick sale real estate transactions, and if they do hold an income property, they are more likely to pay others to do the rehab and to hire a management company to collect rents and deal with tenant issues. The quick, sizable profit is the pursuit in this style of real estate investing.

Of course, many others like to take advantage of the diversity that is offered in real estate. They like to do a little bit of everything. They may buy a fixer upper and do the work themselves, buy properties for a quick resale, and hold various rental properties. These real estate generalists enjoy variety in their work life.

Let's take a closer look at the various ways people make money in the real estate business.

SELLING PROPERTIES

One of the primary ways to make money off of real estate, is obviously to sell it. Good investors who have found bargain properties can make good profits this way, but they have to be careful not to leave themselves to vulnerable to excessive taxation. Investor's increase their profits in the sale of real estate with a variety of strategies:

Appreciation

To enjoy the financial benefits of appreciation, you must be willing to defer the sale of your property until the power of appreciation has done its magic. This is the kind of investing you are doing as a homeowner. Your investment in a home is an investment that will reap rewards in the future through appreciation or the process by which a property's value increases over time via the powers of inflation. Real estate investors also take advantage of appreciation when they buy an income property that they will sell at a later date. The key to making money through appreciation is to buy a bargain house that has a lot of potential. It should have good, solid bones that will see it through the ravages of time. Of course, you will need to do routine maintenance to assure that your house does not develop some serious form of bone cancer. If you are looking to make money via appreciation, you probably want to stay away from modular or mobile homes that tend not to hold up well over time. Appreciation is accelerated through gradual upgrades throughout the year. You must make sure the property keeps up with the neighborhood in which it resides. Holding onto property over the years also offers you protection against inflation and taxes. The best scenario is to buy the house when the market is slow, at a good bargain and then sell when the home has greatly appreciated and that appreciation is further boosted by a market in which your property is in great demand. Over the long haul, you can rely on the market to go up and down.

Fixer uppers:

A common way that people make money in real estate is to buy a property in disrepair for a bargain price and then fix it up to sell at a higher price. This is a good idea, especially if you are handy. Experienced fixer-uppers learn that they shouldn't get too attached to their neglected property. Yes, you can really turn the place into a gem and that can be very emotionally rewarding, but some of those renovations will not add significantly enough to add to the value of your property. Smart rehabbers know that they key is to do strategic refurbishment, and to do it quickly. Each month that you have a vacant property on your hands means that you have a mortgage payment bleeding. You are losing money rather than profiting off of your investment. Investor's specializing in fixers, as they're called, know how to work quickly and to make the most of sweat equity. (See Chapter Eight on Smart Refurbishment.)

Flipping Properties:

A flipper property is one that is bought and quickly resold for a higher price. Flipping properties is an attractive option for investors who don't have the time or inclination to manage properties. The key to making money by flipping properties is to be able to identify really good deals—the properties whose potential others have missed.

In order to make money on a quick resale you must buy a property well below its real market value. To really make it worth your while "Flipper Experts" recommend holding out for properties that can be purchased for 25% or more below the market value. In order to gain that 25% profit, you may have to do some quick fix-up work. You want to make sure that the repairs and upgrades that are necessary are low on cost and labor and high on impact. Flipping properties is a strategy that is most effective if the market is really hot—houses are selling fast and the prices are rising. In such a market, appreciation happens in an accelerated manner, and the investor has to move quickly to avoid delaying sale and encountering an economic down-turn. The "flipper" expert is one who understands the economy and the patterns of the market. With the costs associated with buying and selling (agents commissions, closing costs, attorney's fees, etc), you have to make a fairly steep profit to make it worth your while. Under normal market conditions, a very quick sale may not net you very much over transaction costs. Also, when flipping properties you will probably have to pay higher taxes on your profit and you lose out on the potential income and appreciation that property could generate if it were kept, rented out, and sold at a later date. Still, many investors are in the business of making quick, dramatic profits and quickly reinvesting their earnings. They are not interested in being landlords or doing extensive rehabilitation. They are interested in making deals. Property flippers are usually more experienced real estate investors.

Loan Assumption:

Sometimes you can get a very good deal by taking over a distressed seller's loan, rather than arranging for your own loan and then paying the seller to pay off his or her own debt. Not every loan is assumable, but if it is you may save yourself the costs associated with securing your own loan. You will usually have to pay off the debts that the seller owes as well. The transaction is appealing to the seller simply because they walk away from a sinking ship, finally able to breathe again. Sometimes that is all a distressed homeowner is looking for. Loan assumption makes for a quick sale because it widens the net of potential buyers to include those may not have the money for the costs associated with arranging for a new loan. Of course, not every loan is assumable and you will have to check with the seller's bank or mortgage lender to see if this purchase arrangement is workable. Generally, if you have to pay the seller's debts and penalties *and* pay points and closing costs on a new loan, buying from a financially strapped seller may not be profitable.

Conversions

Say you notice a single family house for sale in a mixed residential and commercial zone. The neighborhood is on an upswing with the trendy coffeeshops, restaurants, bookstores and antique shops doing a brisk business. However, with the new business orientation of the neighborhood, traffic and parking are becoming a problem. There are fewer buyer and renters that want to live in such a busy environment. In such a case, you might find a home priced well, but it may be hard to rent out or resell. In such a case you might make a very healthy profit by converting the home into a commercial space and then renting it out to a business at a higher rent than you could get from a residential tenant. Sometimes a property simply no longer fits into its neighborhood. In such cases, a conversion might lead to a quick spike in rental or selling potential. Sadly, in many areas homeowners are a making a good deal of money selling their property so it can be leveled and turned into parking space. The key to making money on conversions is to take advantage of the changing face of various neighborhoods. It's a "go with the flow" style of investing.

INCOME PROPERTIES

These are often called "keeper properties," in that they aren't being bought with an eye toward immediate resale. Rather, you will enjoy the perks of ownership while generating a rental income. There are many types of properties you can rent out: single family homes, multifamily homes, apartment buildings, apartment complexes, commercial properties, office buildings, and so on. Probably the easiest form of rental for a beginning investor is a single family home. You will only need to deal with one tenant, will probably experience less turnover, there are fewer appliances and systems that can malfunction and you know how to run a family home—you have on of your own. A multi-family home also has its advantages. These might be duplexes or houses that have been irregularly divided. Many split levels have basement apartments, and so on. If you are just starting out, you can live in one part of the property and rent out the other to pay the majority of your mortgage and free up some of your income to invest in other properties. Also, if you have a multifamily property, you won't have to worry so much about vacancy. If you lose a tenant, at least there will be one or more other renters still paying while you find another one. The more units that you have, however, the more potential problems. You have more people to deal with, for one—more personalities, temperaments and potential traumas. You also have more appliances and systems that could break down or be damaged. Buying an apartment building or complex will require much more out of you as a manager, and will cost more to maintain, but could potentially be very profitable. In apartment complexes, dealing with tenants becomes a full time job and you have extras like parking, laundry and perhaps even a swimming pool or common grounds to consider. Office or commercial spaces are generally for the more seasoned real estate investor as these involve more legal entanglements and more risk. A high percentage of businesses fail within the first year, and if the economy falters, the whole area could become persona non grata. Of course, commercial properties also can involve a lot more profit as leases in thriving business areas are sky high. In general, the more risk, the more potential for profit. If you are reading this book, however, you probably are a real estate beginner, and ought to start out with a single family home, a multifamily home, or a small apartment building.

An income property can earn you money in four important ways:

Cash flow: On top of paying your mortgage and all of your other expenses, your income property should provide you with a modest cash flow. When you and your accountant crunch the numbers, this cash flow may be smaller than your had anticipated. After all, there are a lot of operating expenses from routine maintenance, repair work and materials, paying an accountant and maybe even an attorney, taxes and insurance, and so on. However, if you have analyzed the property's potential properly, you should allow for a modest cash flow that will assure, at the very least, that expenses associated with the property do not come out of your pocket. You should have enough to maintain the property nicely and if all goes well you will make a modest yearly profit. Of course, the more properties you own and the more efficiently you fix up and maintain these properties, the more monthly income you will enjoy.

Tax savings: tax law favors ownership. Your accountant will fill you in on the deductions that you will enjoy as your level of property ownership grows. If your career involves owning a property, you aren't going to pay the same percentage of taxes than does somebody working for a regular paycheck.

Equity: Each month that your mortgage is taken out of your monthly income, you are building equity in your property and your net worth grows.

Appreciation: Don't forget that this is the real reason that you have invested in this piece of real estate. If you have purchased a property below market price, the appreciation is instant. But if you hold onto that property your return could increase beyond your greatest expectations, even if you had bought it at market price. You hear about it all the time—people whose property values double or even triple within a decade. After all those years of boosting your monthly income, your property will provide you with a sizeable lump of profit when you finally decide to sell itt, years down the line. This profit can then be leveraged into bolder and more profitable investments and you will begin to experience the snowball effect of financial investing that has created many a millionaire.

Tips for managing properties:

<u>Find a property in an area with plentiful renters and then match your property to the renter market.</u> So for example, if the rental base is college students, hold back on the upgrades and offer inexpensive, extremely durable housing options. Be sure to charge enough to offset summer vacancies, though, and offer incentives for summer occupancy. If there is a nearby business park that employs a lot of entry-level professionals, you can develop more expensive properties with more luxury features, an environment attractive to the young professional single who likes to entertain. In other words, be sure to match your properties with the prevailing renter pool.

<u>Buy only property in good repair and use durable materials</u>. You will lose your shirt on repair work and replacing damaged items if you skimp here. Your tenants will not likely baby your property as a homeowner would. You don't want to have carpets that wear and stain easily, low quality paint that scuffs up, or fixtures that break with heavy use. Go for substance over style.

<u>Choose and prepare properties to minimize maintenance and repair.</u> Big yard? Hot tub? Garbage disposal? Alarm system? Nice features, but each of these represents potential problems for a landlord. You will have to maintain these and fix them when they're broken. Keep it simple.

<u>Buy properties close to where you live.</u> You will be traveling back and forth to attend to business with your properties. Don't spread yourself out over three counties. In fact, it is best to choose a specific neighborhood or area in which to specialize. Real estate experts call this area

your "farm." All your properties should be fairly close together. You can move from one item of business to another quickly and efficiently during your day, and while driving around your area, you can keep tabs on your property. Also, if you specialize in an area, you can be continually "farming"—re-combing that area for deals and opportunities.

Find good tenants. Do a credit check, call former landlords, and verify their income. Of course, you must also trust your instincts and judge potential tenants just as you might an applicant for a job. Are they well groomed, and do they present themselves well? Do they have a fairly steady work history? Do you get the sense that their main occupation is partying?

Treat tenants ethically. When selecting tenants vigilantly assure that you don't discriminate based upon race, religion, age, sexual orientation or some other factor beyond the individual's control. If you have a hunch that a tenant is a bad risk, ask yourself why. If such a judgment is based in bias or stereotype (and we all are subject to these), then try to reassess objectively. You may find that renting to tenants that frequently face discrimination may yield you a long term and loyal tenant. I am a strong believer that being an ethical real estate investor means being successful in the long haul. We know that slumlords can make a lot of money, but they end up with high turnover, lots of damage to their properties, properties that depreciate due to neglect in routine maintenance, and even lawsuits. Only purchase and rent out the number of properties that you can afford to maintain well. Try to treat your tenants with respect. If your properties are pleasant places, you won't have vacancies and your tenants will be more likely to treat your property with respect as well.

At the same time, be businesslike. When you are a landlord, you may find that you develop a somewhat familiar relationship with people. After all, they see you in the context of your home setting. Don't set yourself up for being a parental figure or rental obligations as being somewhat flexible. Create a policy for late rent payments and stick to it. Focus on solutions with clients, rather than listening and sympathizing with their travails. Stick to your policies. Otherwise, you will have dozens of special arrangements with a dozens of different tenants and your business structure will become very chaotic. Make it clear that among financial priorities, shelter has got to be foremost for your tenants.

<u>Set the rents wisely</u>. You want to set your rental prices slightly below the local market price in order to attract renters. However, you need to make sure that you charge your renters the appropriate amount to pay expenses and see a profit each month, even if that profit is not large. Visit your accountant to balance your expenditures against your income and to assure a positive cash flow. If you find you must charge an amount that makes the property prohibitively expensive to rent, then it is a bad investment.

Lease Option:

A lease option can be the best of both worlds—you get both a monthly income boost and the profit associated with a sale. Often the stumbling block for buyers is not the monthly mortgage payment, but rather the initial costs of buying a home. A lease option lets homeowners pay rent to you, but have a certain amount of their rent go toward a down payment on a future purchase of the property. This can be a great thing for both parties. For you, it means a higher monthly rent payment as the tenants are paying a lease option fee on top o f the rent. Renters with a lease option also tend to be very careful with your property as they are hoping that it will one day be their own. You don't have to worry about turn-over and re-renting the place. If the renter decides not to take the option to buy, then you aren't out anything, you can simply re-rent the place.

For a renter/buyer finding a lease option can make the dream of homeownership a reality. They don't have the obstacle of needing a large down payment, closing costs and all the rest all at once and they can test out a property and see if they really like it before exercising their option to buy. This is a serious advantage because a high percentage of home buyers find when they actually take possession of the house and live in it a while, that it really isn't for them. The flow may not be functional for their family; the traffic noise may bother them more than they thought it would, or they may discover that they really aren't country people after all.

5

Secrets of Successful Real Estate Investors

Beyond the basics, what differentiates a real estate investor and the Average Joe is that serious investors know various tricks and strategies that allow them to make more money off of their real estate holdings. For example:

Move In!

Especially at the beginning of your career, you can make even more money if you are flexible about your own living arrangements. Whether it be living on one half of a duplex while renting out the other, or moving into your fixer upper while you rehab, the tax laws favor people buying homes as residences. If you move into the house for two years, you won't have to pay taxes on your profits. You can claim up to $250,000 in tax-free sales profits. (This is currently Internal Revenue Code 121, but always check with your accountant as tax laws are constantly changing.) Many real estate investors, most single or at least without children, make money by buying one home to live in, fixing it up for a big re-sale profit, and then selling it a couple of years later, and buying another fixer upper to rehab. This strategy is clearly not the most popular one for families with children who can't tolerate such disruptions in their lives. Depending upon your personality, you may find this a fun way to go.

Reinvest

Tax laws favor reinvestment. Currently, Internal Revenue Code 1031 allows an investor to sell a property and reinvest the profits in anew property and to defer all capital gains. In plain English, that is less tax money that you pay on your profits. The IRS likes to take money when it is just sitting idle in your bank account. So, before you close the deal and take home that profit, find another property in which to invest it. Keep the ball rolling and you will be amazed how quickly you can become a real estate tycoon.

Finding the real bargains

The real difference between a real estate investor and the rest of us is the real estate investor's ability to find the really good deals. Investors have various strategies they use for finding bargain properties and motivated sellers.

Advertise

As an investor, you want people to come to you so that you don't have to spend all of your precious time searching for investments. You may want to place an advertisement identifying yourself as a real estate investor who is looking to buy properties and make quick and efficient sales. This way, even someone who has not already listed a property, may see your advertisement and a light may go on in their head. They may be having financial problems and see your proposition as a fast way out. They won't have to find and pay an agent and as an investor, you are a sure bet. This way you may find properties before they ever go on the market. Hence, you will have zero competition. Also, you can advertise by word of mouth. When you are strolling through neighborhoods, talking to a banker, calling to inquire about a foreclosure, you are building a network. The larger your network becomes the more efficiently it can help you get the word out: you are a sound real estate investor actively looking for properties. This way, any time someone hears of a property coming up for sale, a family who will have to sell quickly, or someone who is simply thinking of selling, your name will come up. As your career in real estate investing develops, the deals should come to you.

Evaluate the listings

Streamline your search process by developing an eye for good deals. As an investor, you don't want to take the time even to consider the average deal. You are looking for something unique. When browsing through the listings keep your eyes open for:

Properties that have been for sale for quite some time (usually more than 90 days and an agent will be pressuring the seller to take offers.)

Properties that are at a significantly reduced price. This usually will indicate that a seller is motivated. He or she has been unable to sell the property at the asking price. Remember, though, just because a property is selling at a reduced price, doesn't mean that you can't offer less.

Listings that provide hints that "highly motivated seller,"or "Must sell" "flexible terms" are good signs that there is a level of desperation there that will benefit you.

For Sale by Owner

The good thing about going the For Sale by Owner (FSOB) route is that you can negotiate directly with another individual. The two of you can get creative and directly work out a deal that works best for both parties. You can stand face to face and get a sense of each other's priorities. If the seller doesn't want to move out until his retirement a year later, you can save him a lot of trouble and expense by delaying the closing that protracted span of time. After all, you're not waiting to move into the place. In return, he just might give you a real bargain. Or, you can negotiate paying a higher price if he or she will get the place ready for tenant occupancy. Sometimes when working with an agent, you won't get the kind of information about each other that you can by getting together. The real estate agent's priority is getting the highest possible number upon which to base his or her commission. The seller also may be willing to sell at a lower price because he doesn't have that commission to worry about.

Just because the seller is not working with an agent, however, doesn't necessarily mean that you will get a better deal. Some owners who sell their own property do so out of a sort of arrogant innocence. They don't want to pay an agent to sell their home; they can do it themselves and save a lot of money! Without the benefit of an agent's experience and knowledge of the market, such owners may not have a realistic idea of their property's worth and may overcharge.

On the other hand, some sellers handle the sale on their own because they have a good deal of real estate know-how and experience. Many real estate investors do sale by owner transactions. In these cases, the owner knows the value of their property, but may be willing to take a lower price for a quick, uncomplicated sale. FSBO transactions benefit you only if the seller passes on the savings on the agent's commission to you instead of pocketing it.

The more experienced the parties in the FSBO transaction, the less risk is involved in not having an agent. All that paperwork is in play to protect both parties and avoid future legal disputes. Some really experienced investors have all of the processes and legalities down. If you don't feel comfortable with the transaction process without an agent, consider hiring an attorney to handle the transaction for you. This will probably cost at least a thousand dollars, but it will still be less than having the owner tack on a 4–6% increase on the selling price to cover the agent's fees. You can share the attorney's fee with the other party or just negotiate it into the price.

One of the disadvantages of a FSBO is that they may be harder to find. This is one of the key risks that a seller takes when they skip the agent. They won't be on the MLS listing on the Internet, and they obviously won't have agents directing buyers their way. FSBO's rely upon drive-by buyers. As a real estate investor, you should be regularly making the rounds of your "farm" or neighborhoods in which you have identified good bargains in the past. When you see a FSBO sign, jot down the phone number, or stop the car and knock! In choosing not to do business with an agent, the owner has committed him or herself to being bothered by potential buyers. Talk to the owner, but do not reveal too much about the level of *your* motivation. As always, you should adopt a "take it or leave it" attitude toward properties.

Foreclosures and REOs

These can be the holy grail of real estate investors, but the issues involved can be a little bit complicated. If you want to take advantage of foreclosed properties, then you need to understand the foreclosure process and how foreclosed properties are sold. A foreclosure is basically a property in which an owner has lost possession because he or she has not kept up with the mortgage payments. Once the property gets all the way through the foreclosure process it will be owned by the bank. You can buy the property in different stages of the foreclosure process.

If you catch the seller before he or she has entirely lost possession of their property, you have found a very motivated seller. You can often assume their mortgage with very little down, perhaps only making their back payments and paying any penalties they owe so they can walk away from the deal out of debt. If the mortgage is not assumable, then you have to go to the trouble to arrange for a new loan and pay the back payments on the property. In such a case, you have to determine if the deal is worth it. It depends upon just how extensive back payment and penalties have grown. In such cases, you want to be sure to make liberal use of the services of a title company to assure that there are no outstanding liens against the properties. In such cases, the owner's financial troubles are not limited simply to mortgage and they may have other debts that will entangle the transaction. When dealing with properties in foreclosure, prepare yourself for the deal falling apart. Many of them will. Also keep in mind that people in financial trouble may be angry at the bank and may do willful destruction of their own property out of spite, figuring that the bank will own the property soon enough anyway. (Remember Eric and Mya, the young couple who bought a property in foreclosure? In their case, the former tenants had actually set a fire to property outside the house, which had damaged the exterior.) Still you may find that acting the hero and bailing out a troubled homeowner is much less expensive than buying a home from a solvent property owner.

Houses that go into foreclosure are eventually auctioned off, usually for the amount of the loan against it. You have the opportunity to bid on the property, and stand a realistic chance of getting it if you are willing to bid over the loan price. Any bid under that, and the bank will buy it. If nobody buys the house at this juncture, it goes on to become a bank owned property, or an REO, which stands for "real estate owned."

An REO is a different ballgame altogether. Instead of dealing with a distressed homeowner, you will be dealing with a large financial institution whose eyes are on one thing: the bottom line. They are motivated to get rid of properties, but they are not willing to take a loss on the deal. The good news is that the bank's vast store of resources will make the transaction very clean and easy. They know how to take care of the legal end of things, are motivated to get it done quickly and efficiently, and they may even help you with your financing! Still you are not likely to get quite the "steal" you might from a desperate homeowner. Usually banks will clean up a property site and secure it from vandalism, but they do not get too involved in refurbishment and will offer the property "as is." Be sure to have the property carefully inspected to make sure that the required renovations won't outstrip your profit.

How do you find foreclosures and REOs?

This is another secret of the real estate investors. The problem is, you don't always know off the bat if a property is in the foreclosure process. The property may be listed by an agent or might be for sale by owner and you won't initially know that the sellers are highly motivated. Title companies also have lists of properties in foreclosure. The best source for learning about foreclosures is in your local paper. Unfortunately you will not get the street address on these properties from the paper and you will have to call the county assessor's office to get the address, which can be time consuming. If you really know your area, you will be able to sniff out a foreclosure through a variety of methods. You may even know the person published in the paper. If you have a really dynamic and wide ranging network, you will be getting lots of "gossip" to help point you to foreclosures—neighbors, real estate agents, bankers, even your local handyman. If you get the word out, people will even contact you themselves. Once you do identify an individual going through foreclosure, give them a call. They may be a little bit disgruntled about it and may even view your call as an intrusion, but when they realize that you could be the answer to their problem, they will take your number and call you, if they don't take the bite upon the first contact.

REOs can be even harder to find. They aren't generally advertised. You will have to call the bank and ask to speak with the official in charge of REOs. Oftentimes, banks don't want to bother with your average public buyers and only correspond with what they consider legitimate investors. As a real estate investor you will want to develop a relationship with various lenders so that they will disclose their REOs to you and be willing to deal with you. Once you have developed this relationship you are in a wonderful position to find good deals that are quickly done.

Homes at Auction

Mary is eighty-five years old and has recently been placed in a nursing home because she has gone blind. This is a sad situation, but a common one. It is also a great opportunity for a real estate investor. Mary's children are placing her house and most of its contents up for auction in order to pay the mounting nursing home bills. Families in such positions will generally hire an auction house to perform the sale for them. Get to know your local auction houses and keep track of their upcoming auctions. If you see a property that interests you, you will need to offer a great deal up front to secure the property, so you will want to start the process before the day of the auction. Go view the property and if you like it, get your financing in line. Determine how much you will pay for it and then be prepared to spend a long day at auction. Many real estate investors find these to be rather fun, however, and often also pick up valuable items like appliances and building supplies that they need in their business.

Government Repossessions

Any government program that provides funding for home ownership will have a storehouse of repossessions from people who have failed to live up to their terms. Whether it is HUD, or the VA or the FHA, these agencies likely have a good number of properties up for sale and there may be one in your area. The only way to find out is to call each of these agencies individually to find out.

6

Evaluating Properties

Whether you are looking for a house to occupy yourself, a house to refurbish and sell at a profit or one to rent out now and sell at a much later date, the key to making money in real estate is buying a property that will have greater value in the future. You want a property that has the potential for solid appreciation and one that will be appealing to buyers, regardless of when you plan to sell. With any property, someday you will be selling it, and you don't want to find yourself unable to do so because you weren't thinking of resale when you bought.

It may seem counter-intuitive, but the time to assure that you will make the best profit on your investment, is not when you *sell* it, but when you *buy* it. If you are buying the property just for investment purposes, you want to make sure that you buy the property for less than it is actually worth. That is the business of real estate investing. Your job is to sniff out the out-of-the-ordinary deal and pass on the regular deals. (If you are buying the home to occupy, you may be satisfied to get a home priced in sync with the market, but as a real estate investor you must expect more than that.) In order to assure that you are paying at or below market rates, you must carefully monitor the real estate market in your area. Real estate investors continually check list prices in the paper and on the Internet. They develop relationships with talkative agents and brokers, ask neighbors how much houses are going for in the area, and so forth. Most of us have probably chatted with a real estate investor on a fact-finding mission without even knowing it.

Your attitude during the house hunt will of course differ depending upon whether it will be your home or strictly an investment. After all, your emotions will be prominently involved if you are planning to place your little toddler in the front bedroom and your great grand-mother's armoire in the living room. However, in any instance you must keep your emotions in check and do a thorough appraisal of every potential property. You are always looking for a *good buy* and that must be the bottom line. What makes a good buy in real estate?

A good price from a motivated seller.

A fixer-upper that primarily requires sweat equity. (paint, cleaning, and landscape clean-up, for example)

A low interest rate loan.

For investment properties, as little down as possible.

If you are evaluating a property to be your own personal residence, you will have more difficulty remaining objective and making smart deci-sions. Often, people make their biggest investing mistakes on their first home. This can prevent people from realizing the promise of real estate investing, or it can prompt them to be smarter as they evaluate their next property. To avoid making a costly and impulsive real estate deci-sion, even if you are searching for your cherished first home, you must strive to maintain a balances perspective of desirable features, utility and resale. Chances are your first home will not be the one in which you retire. I don't mean that you should ignore your inner voice—your "hunch" that tells you that this house *feels* like home. It is absolutely essential that a house *feel* right to you. However, this is a transaction that will have a huge impact upon your daily life for many years to come and a huge impact on your financial future and you must have more to go on than a hungh.

Lisa and Greg's story is very typical of many people's first experience of homeownership. They had been renters for a long time. When they had their first child, they began to feel insecure about the tenuous nature of the lease and weary of the landlord's habit of stopping in unannounced. As nature demands, the young couple began to recognize their need for a nest to call their own. As a young single income family, they had a modest approval price and were getting a little discouraged viewing the older homes with cramped rooms and a general state of disrepair that were in their price range. They just couldn't see their baby crawling around and growing up in these musty and cramped properties. When they walked into 18 Floral Avenue, however, the first thing that caught their eye was the clean plush carpeting that seemed to spread out for miles throughout the spacious, open floor plan. Lisa's face brightened as she hugged her baby and exclaimed, "This is it!" With their encouraged real estate agent, they toured the house, gasping with appreciation and relief. "The paint color is so cute in here!" "The brick patio is charming!" "It really *flows*!" "And it's so clean!" Indeed, it was a house with many favorable characteristics, and believe me, the real estate agent was left with a solid impression that that the couple *just had to have* this house. They put in their offer that day and moved in three months later.

It turned out, however, that this transaction was one that Lisa and Greg would ultimately regret. The emotions, issuing from their disappointment with the properties they had recently viewed, the protective feeling they had for their child, and their dreams of home ownership, allowed them to overlook a number of features of this particular home:

The house was situated on a street with a heavy traffic flow.

The house had only one bathroom and no bathroom at all upstairs where the bedrooms were.

The kitchen was badly in need of remodeling and had no dishwasher.

There was no heat upstairs.

The house was being encroached upon on two sides by dilapidated student housing.

The house was listed with the same real estate firm for which the Lisa and Greg's agent worked.

For these features, Lisa and Greg probably paid more than the house was worth. However, their real estate agent had known that their hearts were set on the house, and this information no doubt found its way to the agent's long time friend and colleague, the seller's agent.

In two years, Lisa and Greg found themselves hosting an open house. Lisa was fed up with washing dishes by hand; their cat had already been killed on the busy street, and having to come down the stairs every time they had to go to the bathroom in the middle of the night was becoming a little more than an inconvenience. Lisa and Greg didn't have the money for the improvements that would have made the home more livable. Because of the undesirable location, Lisa and Greg did not end up making a profit on their sale, and they had to re-raise much of the down payment and the closing costs on their next home purchase. You can bet that on their next house hunt, Lisa and Greg poured all their powers of concentration into thoroughly evaluating the property. They left their daughter with her grandmother and got themselves into a more business-like frame of mind. When they found a house and decided to make an offer, their real estate agent didn't even see it coming. Now they have a smart investment and a home that they enjoy. They will eventually see a great return on their investment.

In order to make a wise home purchase, you need to arm yourself with information, and fully consider a range of issues. Don't see too many houses in one day. You need to have all of your skills of concentration at the ready. Bring a notebook to write down various features of the home so that you will remember all of the variables later. These issues will affect your experience in the home, and the home's potential for resale or tenant occupancy. As you tour homes, keep these issues in mind:

Consider how much will the home cost you to maintain or fix up for sale. A bargain price is not a bargain if you have to pump a lot of money into the house once it's yours. A good home inspector will help you to evaluate the repairs that are necessary, but since a home inspection can be expensive, you want to consider these factors yourself before you put in an offer.

> What renovations will be needed to keep the house livable for you? (Do you find the kitchen too small? Do you intensely dislike the dated tiles in the bathroom?) What will need to be done to assure that the house will sell at the right price?
>
> How is the water pressure? Check faucets and flush toilets. When was the plumbing last replaced?
>
> What appliances will you need to buy? How new are the appliances?
>
> How about the electrical system? Check all outlets, light switches, and lights.
>
> How old is the roof? Of what material is it made?
>
> Any signs of leaks?
>
> Are there any trees that will need to be trimmed regularly to keep branches off the roof?
>
> How big is the yard? Do you have the time and the equipment needed to maintain it?
>
> Is there a pool that will need to be maintained?

If you are buying the house to live in yourself, you must ask how much it will cost to get the house up to speed for your requirements. If you are buying the house to re-sell, the issues will be similar, but keep in mind the buyers may be more open to making cosmetic improvements to tailor the house to their own tastes.

Is the neighborhood desirable?

I remember when my husband and I were searching for a new apartment to rent while we were in graduate school. We had gotten very discouraged when we looked at property after property in the lovely neighborhoods near the park and near the University: tiny, filthy little things that we could barely afford. Feeling thoroughly dejected, we responded to an advertisement for an apartment on the second floor of a row house downtown. We couldn't believe our eyes and the price when we arrived. Beautiful wood floors, crown moulding, and the kitchen lovingly restored by the landlord who lived upstairs. The place was filled with features that renters usually have to do without: laundry in the unit, heated floors in the bathroom, a garbage disposal. The little patio in the back was ornately landscaped to disguise the urban view and give a sense of a peaceful oasis. We signed a lease right then and there. We simply couldn't believe the price and our good fortune. Well, it *was* a great place, and I have good memories of it. However, perhaps we should have spent a little more time evaluating the neighborhood. This was a very distressed neighborhood—a laundramat occupied the space just below us and a liquor store was next door. The area could be fairly described as a slum. Sure, there was a park a few blocks away, and we used this as a factor which mitigated the urban blight issue, but when we walked there, we invariably received menacing stares and comments—people thought we were undercover cops! The laundramat downstairs provided plentiful noise and entertainment—fights and drunken revelry, not to mention the steady hum of those heavy duty appliances. The liquor store was a favorite hangout for the youth of the area, out smoking "blunts" and listening to loud music. Worst of all, just under our bedroom window, cars pulled up at night pumping a jarring baseline, staying a while and then roaring off, only to be replace by another a short time later. This would go on all night. We soon realized that beneath our window, in the parking lot of the liquor store, was a favorite spot for drug dealers to make transactions. Not exactly a peaceful night's sleep! When visitors came to see us, they often had their cars broken into or vandalized in some manner. Luckily we didn't have children. There was no safe place for children to play, and I am sure the schools were troubled. Needless to say, the garbage disposal started to lose its seductive power. We didn't re-up our lease the following year. While this is an extreme example of a youthful lack of impulse control (thank heavens we weren't buying), there are plentiful tales of young buyers, so entranced by the luxury features of a home that they don't consider the neighborhood.

If the home stands out from those around it and is clearly the nicest property in the neighborhood, be warned. You cannot fix up the neighborhood to match the house. That is why it is commonly advised to buy the worst property in a good neighborhood. This is especially the case when you are buying a property strictly for its investment potential. Such a property will probably be well priced, and you can fix that property up to bring it up to speed with the quality of the surrounding properties. A neighborhood in decline is a risky proposition. Chances are, it will get worse and you will have a great deal of trouble re-selling the house regardless of the features of that house or the improvements that you have made.

Before you even see the house, as you are driving up, look around you. What are the conditions of the other houses in the area? Do they reflect a pride of ownership? Or are you seeing boarded up windows, junk cars in the driveway and lawns choking on weeds? Even if you find a nice street that seems well kept up, drive around a little to get a sense of the neighborhood borders. Neighborhoods in decline tend to swallow up surrounding neighborhoods in due time. It is a sad truth. This also serves to remind property owners that everyone on the block has a part to play in keeping neighborhoods alive and vital, and keeping property values steady. Doing the required maintenance and upkeep on your home is not just your business. It is the civic-minded thing to do. Those flowerboxes on your front porch have more power than you might expect.

What is the crime rate in the area?

This one is intertwined with the overall quality of the neighborhood, but sometimes you can be surprised. A very quaint neighborhood can have a crime problem. I remember when I was house hunting once, there was a particular neighborhood that I found especially appealing. It had trendy coffee shops, unique casual restaurants, and a very pretty park across the street. Well, the park was nice, but it was a wonderful hang out place for the criminal element. Luckily, I had been reading the crime blotter on a regular basis. I kept reading about people being hit over the head with lead pipes or other blunt instruments and then robbed—all on my darling little street. I looked elsewhere. Track the crime statistics in the local paper for a while, but also get information by talking to people in the neighborhood and seeing what borders the area in question. Parks look nice, but are often crime ridden, and a nice neighborhood can often get a lot of pedestrian traffic from an undesirable neighborhood, depending upon what path such traffic takes in your community. A home in an area with a crime problem can still sell, but it will be less likely to sell to retirees, single women or people with children, or so statistics suggest. You don't need your list of potential buyers to be so circumscribed from the outset.

What is the quality of the neighborhood school and how does it compare with the other schools in the area?

If you have very young children or no children at all, this may not be an issue that you place very high on your priority list. However, even if you never plan to have any children at all, this is a very important factor in determining the investment potential of your home. When you send that tiny tot off to kindergarten, believe me, you will be willing to move hell or high water to send them to the best place. The way people feel about their children, they will be willing to pay much higher housing costs and go to great lengths to get their children into a good school. People relocate, send their children to private schools, pay extra taxes just to find the best education for their kids. If you find a lovely home in an area that has a notoriously bad school, then when it comes time to sell it, families with children or couples who plan to have children will generally steer clear—even if it does have a hot tub and new granite countertops! The quality of school in the area is probably the single most powerful influence upon the property values in that area.

So how do you know about the quality of the schools? Well, you can check test scores and other statistics online, but these numbers don't always tell the story. The best way to get the full story is to talk to as many people as you can. Nobody likes to feel that their child is going to a substandard school, so if you just ask one opinion, that person may offer a rose-colored vision of the quality of the school their children attend. "Sure it's a great school! My kids love it!" Try to see the forest through the trees by asking a lot of different types of people—ask real estate agents, parents, grandparents who have lived in the area a long time, bankers…get a wide cross section of opinion. Usually there is community lore that paints a clear picture of which schools are considered the best and which are not to be considered. In our area, for example, there is one school that elicits raised eyebrows from almost everyone you ask. Our realtor said it best, "If you find a house in that area, you have to factor in the cost of private school." Property near the best school in town will be the most valuable. Buyers will know that they can always fix up the property they find in the right area, but they can't fix the damage done to their child if they end up in a bad school district.

Is the house in close proximity to convenient services and shopping?

When sizing up a property, look carefully at the surrounding area—what might draw a potential buyer? Is there a new business park nearby and might the home be attractive for eliminating a commute for someone who works there? Are there opportunities for entertainment or leisure nearby? Are there nice neighborhood restaurants, a video store, a dry cleaners, a coffee shop? Any nightlife? If there is an up and coming business district nearby, then it is possible that even a neighborhood in disrepair might be on the upswing. For a real estate investor on the prowl for a really good bargain, sometimes a property in a distressed neighborhood that is in the process of recovery is the best deal of all. In ten years, maybe it will be a prize address for a new wave of young business professionals.

These days many people are fed up with long commutes. They like to be close to work and be able to "pop out" to rent movies or buy a few groceries. If your house is on a quiet street and yet it is really in the center of the action, it will be appealing to a lot of buyers.

After a while, the real estate investor will become an expert on most of these issues in their community. As a professional property hunter, you will be the one to ask about neighborhoods, crime rates, and schools and typical housing prices because you will make it your business to know, each and every day. Real estate investors have to know a lot about the communities in which they will be investing. But that alone won't lead the real estate investor to the really good deal.

<u>The single greatest factor in the pursuit of the good real estate deal lies in **the motivation of the seller**.</u>

The simple truth is that people will be willing to take less money for their property, if they are really itching to get out. Sometimes a quick, uncomplicated sale is more valuable to people than a high profit margin. As a professional real estate investor, oftentimes you will get a great deal simply because of your ability to buy quickly and save the seller months of having agents and prospective buyers tromping through their living room. This is just what many sellers are looking for. Some sellers are under a great deal of pressure to sell, and are willing to take a below market price because it is worth it to them to have the whole process over and done with quickly. They cannot afford to wait. It is an unfortunate reality in real estate that someone else's misfortune is often your good luck. Some reasons a seller might be very motivated include:

Financial troubles: Often homeowners find they have bitten off more than they can chew financially. Each month they sink deeper into debt with a mortgage too high for their income. They need to halt this process *quickly*, before they find themselves facing foreclosure or bankruptcy. Often these homes reflect the emotional state of the owner and are in a state of neglect. This will drive the price down as well. However, often this neglect is only as a result of a few months in which maintenance was not done and a poor job done in the move-out clean-up process. Such disrepair is fairly easy and cost efficient to reverse.

Death: When a family member dies, the family often is forced to suddenly rearrange their lives. The surviving spouse may find that they can no longer afford the mortgage or that they wish to move away, closer to their extended family. A family who has inherited a property may want to turn it into liquid cash quickly to settle family disputes over ownership or simply to have the painful ordeal settled.

Divorce: If you've ever been forced to live with someone you hate, you will understand the urgency with this one. In order to separate, a couple may need to sell their house to divide the assets. The less time it takes, the less pain need be endured.

Job Transfer: When someone gets a new job opportunity, there usually is not a long waiting period before it begins. Families will often have to move and then sell their home from a distance. Or, one spouse may move ahead of time and leave the other to settle business. They may be desperate to sell to get themselves reunited and resettled.

Management problems: Some people just aren't cut out for real estate. In the case of an income property like an apartment or office building, an owner might be eager to sell because he or she cannot tolerate the management responsibilities that are associated with the property. Maybe they don't like getting constant phone calls about tenant disputes or repairs. Maybe the upkeep of the property is more costly than they had envisioned and their inability to do needed repairs is causing unrest on the part of the tenants. If you feel you can better handle the duties of this unprepared landlord, the property may come to you at a reasonable price.

Partnership problems: This is sort of like a divorce in an income property. Oftentimes investors buy real estate in partnership with someone else, and when the partnership goes sour, they both want to get out fast.

One word of caution regarding the "distressed seller." There may be a good reason the seller is so eager to get rid of the property. You could very well end up distressed as well if you buy such a property. This is why it is important that you try to uncover the reason for a seller's high level of motivation. If the seller is eager to unload the property at a bargain price because the plumbing and electrical systems are totally shot, then that good deal doesn't look as sweet. If a landlord wants to sell a property because he can't keep it rented out due to an undesirable location, it is very likely you would have the same problem. In looking at the seller's motivation, you must determine that the situation would be entirely different for you.

When you have selected a property that looks like a good deal in the three important areas of market price, location, and seller motivation, then it is time to ring up your accountant for some more complicated math. As a real estate investor, your accountant will end up being an important person in your life. Rather than simply relying on a "hunch" that you will make out like a bandit with this property, your accountant can calculate, with a fair degree of certainty, whether or not the property will be a wealth bonanza or a cash drain. Your accountant, especially if they specialize in real estate, will be able to run a thorough financial analysis on the property, much like the analysis that your financial planner does with your investments. He will calculate expenses associated with the property, probably rates of appreciation, taxes and income to be generated. As you develop a relationship with your accountant, he or she can act fairly quickly on your behalf to make sure that you are able to move quickly on good real estate deals.

You want to receive good terms when you purchase each property. You want to have a low down payment and a good monthly rate, however, you should beware of deals that sell properties above market price, trying to lure borrowers with good terms. Be sure that you know the market and can determine how a property is priced in relationship with similar properties in the area. You don't want to buy an $80,000 property for a $100,000, even if it is "no money down!" Because there are so many amateurs in the real estate business, there are also lots of entrepreneurs out there hoping to make money off of their ignorance.

Consider the neighborhood and local trends. The location of the home will have a lot to do with the resale value of your home. It also may greatly affect the enjoyment that you experience in the home. You may fall in love with a house that has luxury features at a bargain, but in the long run, being stuck in a "turkey" of a neighborhood far away from the people and places you enjoy, and even those hardwood floors can't make up for that feeling of being stranded. Location is a very important factor that smart buyers consider when deciding whether or not to purchase a home. If you see a house that seems to have been on the market forever, chances are it is in an undesirable location. So step outside of the house itself and ask yourself some questions:

How busy is the street?

Does the neighborhood seem to be on the upswing or on the decline?

How is the local economy?

Are there a wide variety of employers in the area or is the area over dependent upon one major employer? (And how secure is that employer?)

How does the house compare to its neighbors? Is it a nice house in a run down neighborhood? Or is it a run-down house in a nice neighborhood? (It is easier to spruce up your home to match a nice neighborhood than to hope that your neighbors will spruce up theirs.)

Consider your needs. Sometimes a house will grab your fancy, but after a year of living there, you discover a plethora of ways that the house doesn't fit.

How much space do you need? You want a house that doesn't feel cramped, gives your family room to grow, gives you the number of rooms that you need. At the same time, you don't want a lot of extra square footage that you won't actually need, space that you'll have to heat and furnish and clean.

How usable is the space? Mentally go through your daily routine to see if there may be any usability problems. Will you have to hike through the garage and up a flight of stairs to unload groceries? Is the kitchen right next to the master bedroom? Will you be waking up your late-sleeping spouse as you do your morning cooking routine? Will you be close enough or too close to your children at night? Will you be able to oversee what is going on in one major area while you are in another? Will you be able to work in the kitchen while watching the kids play safely outside?

Is the location good for you? Are you in a neighborhood that you enjoy? Is your commute to work manageable or is it going to take up too much of your valuable time?

Once you have found a house that seems in good repair and within your maintenance tolerance, is in a favorable neighborhood and seems to "fit" the way you or your family needs to live…and if on top of all that it *feels like home,* then it is time to make an offer. If the home is an investment property and it appeals to you, it will also appeal to renters and future buyers. The important thing is to separate out your particular needs and desires from those that may not overlap with a majority of potential buyers and renters. A good investment buy is one that will appeal to the largest possible number. So, for example, if you just love the corrugated metal on the ceiling of this house, great! But do consider how many other people share this aesthetic and if you are willing to have it redone to make a sale.

7

The Number's Game:
Negotiations and Mortgages

Remember that when you are buying a property, whether it be a home for yourself or an investment, you are entering into a negotiation. You want to pay the lowest possible price for the property and the seller, of course, wants to sell at the highest possible price. So, as friendly and amiable a person as you may be, you are still entering into a transaction in which you and the other party are at cross-purposes. If you have a real estate agent, neither of you will be negotiating on your own behalves. However, a professional real estate investor will often bypass the real estate agent to avoid paying the high sales commissions and so, if you want to really make it as a real estate investor, you have to become a good negotiator.

In the case of the purchasing a home for yourself and your family to live in, many owners and buyers never even meet until the closing. This is why your choice of a real estate agent is so important. You want to assure that your agent is on your side and they are motivated to help you get the best possible deal. Even with the best real estate agent in town, you don't want to be a hapless pawn in the process.

The most serious lapses in negotiation strategy usually happen to inexperienced homebuyers who are buying a home to live in themselves, perhaps even their first home. Buying a home is a very emotional process and many homebuyers really let their emotions wreak havoc on their negotiations. If you are vulnerable to this pitfall, then prepare yourself carefully before the negotiation process. Do an objective appraisal of the local market the pros and cons of the location on your own, and then be prepared to hold your cards in close as you view properties and talk to sellers and agents.

Remember Lisa and Greg? Do you have your heart absolutely set on a property? Don't let your agent know this. They may communicate to the seller's agent that this buyer is "very motivated" to buy the property. In other words: "You don't have to budge an inch on the selling price; they'll meet it." Are you willing to pay $120,000, but are going to offer $115,000? Don't reveal how high you will go. You want the sellers and their agent to think that they may lose the sale if they don't take the offer. In relationships, it may be admirable to wear your heart on your sleeve, but in business, your emotions are usually used against you. If you communicate the attitude that you really could take or leave the property, this places you in the most powerful bargaining position. This can't be all bluff, either. You must be willing to walk away from a bad deal.

You also need to assess the homeowner's bargaining position. Can they take or leave your offer? Are they willing to just sit and enjoy their lovely home until someone comes along and offers their inflated price? Remember, the bargain hunting homebuyer's bread and butter is the *distressed homeowner*. This is somebody who cannot just smugly take or leave an offer. Sometimes your real estate agent will lead you to a distressed seller or will have information about the motivation of the seller that may help you. Other times, you will have to find such information out yourself. The seller's agent, of course, wants to mask these signs of distress. It is a bit of a game, isn't it? Just do me one favor: don't you play the distressed buyer! Believe me, it will be held over you in the bargaining process. So be cool, calm and collected.

If you plan to offer less than the list price, then have a justification at the ready. This information will likely get passed onto the seller and it may convince him or her that the house is unlikely to sell at the list price in light of the issue brought up by the homeowner. Clearly communicate to your agent or directly to the seller (in writing preferably) that you must offer less than the full price, and then provide as many solid reasons as you can. For instance:

The home has an inadequate number of rooms. You'll have to add another bathroom or build on space for another bedroom.

The patio is crumbling which constitutes a safety problem. It will have to be redone.

The roof is on the brink of needing to be redone.

The taxes are high.

The home is in a flood zone and any buyer will have to also budget for flood insurance.

The home is in a bad school district and money will have to be budgeted for private school.

Remember, negotiation is a game based in argument. If you can convince the homeowner that they may have trouble selling the house, you will be in a better position.

While you may feel very emotionally attached to a certain property, try to maintain your common sense. Be willing to walk away if the terms aren't right for you. You will find another house in which you feel "at home." Perhaps even moreso. It never hurts to make an offer that is too low if you really and truly aren't willing to pay what the seller is asking. You may get a wonderful deal, and if not, you haven't lost anything. You wouldn't have been able to afford it anyway.

Other factors to consider in the bargaining process:

What are the inclusions? Do the appliances come with the property? How about that hot tub? Window treatments? Be sure to list all the inclusions that you want when your agent writes up the offer. You don't want to be surprised on move-in day to find that you have no appliances, that the build in speakers have been torn out of the walls, and that you need to put up sheets to cover the windows from the eyes of prying neighbors. Extra inclusions can be used as bargaining chips. Say you'll move up your offer price by a thousand if they throw in the moveable wet bar they had planned to take with them. (You would have paid the extra thousand anyway, but they don't need to know that.) Each purchase that you need to make after closing is part of the price of buying the home.

<u>Closing Date.</u> Usually both parties don't completely agree on what moving day would be most convenient. This is another subject for negotiation. If you agree to a higher price, they could agree to a closing date that is most convenient for you. If they agree to accept a lower offer, maybe you can use the fact that they need to stay in the home 'til the end of the school year as a negotiating chip. You agree to a later closing date in return for a reduced price. Selling a home is very stressful, if you make it easier for the seller, you may be able to get a price reduction.

Don't be discouraged or offended if your offer is met with a counter-offer. Remember, this is business. Simply consider on what terms you are willing to bend and how much. If you and the seller cannot agree on terms, then move on. However, I can guarantee that there will come a day that you will get the call…"Your offer has been accepted."

Ok, so now you have found the house you want, the seller has agreed to your terms and you are ready to go…to the bank, that is. No matter what pre-approval you have received, you have not gone through the actual, sometimes long and agonizing application process. You have just ended a negotiation process with the seller, and now you must be prepared to enter another negotiation process…this time with a major financial institution. You may or may not have felt intimidated by negotiations with a real estate seller, but in that case, you were negotiating with an individual—perhaps someone very much like you that had the same apprehensions and level of naivetÈ about the process. Now, however, you will be negotiating with pros. They have a lot more power and are a lot more intimidating. But you have something on your side. They need your business, and you can simply stand up and walk out of their office and into another office if you don't like what is going on. Your action multiplied by hundreds of others like you, and this is the kind of power that can bring a major financial institution to its knees. A lender's dream come true is an ignorant customer. When you are such a customer, they can sit down and smile while you initial and sign to terms that the bank likes and that you don't understand. In order to get the best deal and the best terms on your mortgage, you absolutely have to be an informed consumer. Thanks to the Internet, you can walk into the bank with a list of the terms that you want—terms you could get elsewhere—and a deep familiarity with the process.

When comparison-shopping, however, don't make the mistake of filling out multiple applications. Find out the terms and compare those, but don't set yourself up for all those application fees. You should be able to get an idea about the terms that should be available for you online or by talking to various lenders. Remember, you are a consumer in this transaction and there are lenders competing for your business. So, do your homework and shop around when looking for a mortgage.

If you don't shop around and just surrender yourself to one institution you can find yourself with unfavorable terms that could cost you a great deal over the life of your mortgage. Oftentimes, first time buyers are so eager to be homeowners, that a financial institution that can make it happen for them are in a position to take tremendous advantage by locking in terms that they don't fully understand. So, understand the following *terms,* and shop around to see if you can find better ones:

Interest Rates:

Interest is a fee, a percentage paid on an annual basis, that the lender charges for the use of its funds. Interest rates are closely tied to the economy and the "going rate" changes depending upon economic conditions. When you are applying for a mortgage, you have to decide if you want a loan with an interest rate that changes as the economy does ("adjustable"), or a "fixed rate" mortgage that locks you in at a specific interest rate. There are a variety of options out there in terms of how interest rates are handled.

Fixed rate: With this type of mortgage, you are able to "lock in" a specific interest rate and therefore, you will always have the same monthly payment. You can see why they call this type of mortgage "a hedge against inflation." Of course, the best time to obtain a fixed rate mortgage is when interest rates are low and you expect that they will be going up in the future.

Adjustable Rate Mortgage (ARM): With this type of mortgage, your interest rate will go up and down in synchronicity with general market interest rates. Usually, the ARM is offered as a fixed rate for a period of six months to several years, and then after that the rate adjusts with market rates. You do have some protection against skyrocketing interest rates as often the lender will create "ceiling caps" or limits to how much your interest rate can rise on an annual basis. These mortgages are attractive to some because the initial interest rate can be lower than the going fixed rate. These are a bit like the 0% interest credit card offers. They tempt you with a low opening rate, figuring they will make their money back later. While general financial wisdom favors the fixed rate, especially for people with low risk tolerance (which is the condition of most first time buyers), some people argue that an ARM is a viable option for those who are not planning to live in their current home for very long, and so the opening low rate may balance out higher rates for the few years that follow the initial period.

Fixed and variable combination mortgages: These mortgages are usually divided into two terms. You pay a certain interest rate for a portion of your mortgage (usually five or seven years), and then a different rate for the remainder of your mortgage (23 or 25 years). Sometimes you can obtain a loan that is fixed for one period and an ARM for the next.

FHA Mortgage: The Federal Housing Administration is a division of the federal government whose aim it is to open the doors to home ownership to more people. An FHA loan is a good option for people who have problems with their credit rating and/or who will have trouble coming up with down payment or closing cost funds. FHA standards are more relaxed than those applied to conventional mortgages. With an FHA Mortgage you may be able to purchase a house with as little as 3% down. They may allow you to carry a higher percentage of your income as housing costs than a bank would, and may allow higher debt to income ratios as well. They also are more likely to lend to folks with bruised credit. FHA mortgages give people who may be denied the privilege of home ownership through private institutions another chance. And what is even more encouraging is that the interest rates for FHA loans are generally the same as for other loans.

Length of Mortgage:

Another choice you will be making when you apply for a mortgage is just how long you will be paying a mortgage. The most popular choices are 15-year and 30-year mortgages. Of course, with a 15-year mortgage, your monthly payments will be significantly higher. Many first time homebuyers are not in a position to even consider a 15 year mortgage, and the option may not even be presented to you. The 15-year mortgage is generally a half a percentage rate lower in terms of interest rate, and because you are accumulating interest for half the time, the shorter mortgage period can save you thousands of dollars in the long run.

For example, say you signed on for a $150,000 dollar mortgage for 15 years at 6.5% interest. You would pay $309 dollars more per month than if you had signed up for a 30-year mortgage at 7%. That's pretty significant. But, if you fast forward, you will see that that extra $309 dollars per month would save you $124,020 on the total cost of your home. Imagining yourself with free and clear ownership of your home in 15 years, with a $124,020 savings, makes that $309 dollars per month seem like a pretty good investment. In fact, if most of us committed to a cost saving measure like driving a used car rather than financing a new one for $300 or so a month, a 15 year mortgage suddenly becomes more viable. If you do not plan on holding onto the property for a very long time, then you should go with the longer mortgage, but for a homeowner a 15 year mortgage can be a smarter way to invest.

A financial lender wants to assure that you will not over-extend yourself and end up defaulting on your obligation to them. Therefore, they establish a certain limits on your monthly housing costs in proportion to your income and your existing debt. Your monthly housing costs are made up of your mortgage principle, interest, taxes and insurance—(and all of these are taken care of by sending one lump sum to your lender.) A good rule of thumb to avoid getting yourself in over your head is never to take on a monthly mortgage cost that is more than 25% of your monthly take home pay. However, some lower income folks are forced to spend a larger ratio of their income on home ownership and this may be a wise use of one's meager funds. Programs like the FHA mortgage give lower income buyers the right to do so.

The first mortgage you get is always the hardest. You are establishing yourself with a financial institution, and once you do so, you will more easily find financing in the future. The more experience you have as a real estate investor, the more easily and quickly you'll be able to find financing for your investments. Many seasoned real estate investors are able to act at lightening speed when they find a bargain property. This gives them a serious advantage over new homebuyers. With our first house, for example, the process took over four months between the offer and the closing. So, if you are in such a position, comfort yourself in the knowledge that the mortgage application process is always the hardest the first time.

When you have found a mortgage with good terms and you feel you fully understand it's short and long term implications, it is time to fill out the application, and that is not a simple task. When you have completed the application and have attached all the necessary materials, you will have a thick folder of paperwork and you may just feel that you have just been unnecessarily tortured as some sort of initiation ritual. That may be just a little bit true, but the bank is also considering a wide range of factors when deciding whether or not to approve a mortgage application. The bank is looking to answer questions such as the following:

What is your credit history?

What is your savings history?

What is your monthly income?

What debt load are you carrying?

How long have you been in your current job?

How economically stable are you?

All of these factors create a picture of risk for the bank. The better you can look in these categories, the more easily you will acquire a mortgage. But don't fear. People with imperfect credit do get approved for mortgages. As do people with modest incomes, sizeable debt, and people who have recently switched jobs. The point is that you don't want to look like a risky bet on all counts. Whatever you can do to improve the picture, do so.

Along the way, you may run into a bump or two. The bank may require additional information or place an added requirement upon you. If a bank has a question, you may be required to write a letter of explanation. I know one couple, Ann and Mark, who applied for a mortgage and in the agonizing eight week approval process they were required to write two letters: one explaining why Ann had taken six month's time off from her job in the last four years (the birth of two children) and another explaining why Mark had changed jobs so frequently (graduate school and internships). They also were required to take out a loan on his 401K earnings in order to establish that they had their own money since their down payment was a gift from a family member. Ann and Mark felt like they'd been through the wringer when it was all done, but they got their house in the end. As I emphasized before, banks are no longer searching out reasons to reject people. In many instances, they are searching out justification to approve people. Ann and Mark may have looked like a questionable risk, but when the bank got the whole picture, they seemed like a better risk. After all, Mark had invested in a graduate education, and taking time off from work to care for a newborn child is not exactly a sign of irresponsibility. (Although it is a problem that mortgage lenders don't value family-oriented decisions more highly. Women especially find that when they decide to stay at home with their children, banks don't usually see this as a sign of stability and an investment in the future. They only tend to see the bottom line—the income level—and they don't factor in the costs of daycare or the emotional costs to the family.) You should however, anticipate, what sort of risk picture you will be on paper, and then see what ways you can put that in context. You may find that successfully negotiating the mortgage process is a satisfying learning experience in itself.

8

Smart Refurbishment

For homeowners, one way to make your property appreciate even faster is to make improvements over the years. Keep in mind that certain improvements will pay off in resale value moreso than others. Getting luxurious white carpeting may seem wonderful to you, but chances are, by the time you sell the place, it will need to be replaced, and even if your habits are so scrupulous that the carpet gleams upon resale, the family with the two kids and the dog may feel a bit squeamish about their ability to keep it white. Hardwood floors, on the other hand, are a feature that is very appealing to many buyers and they generally have great longevity. Their appeal will still shine when it comes time to resell, and the buyer knows the same will be true for them. Adding a bathroom or an extra bedroom is usually an improvement that pays off big in resale. Kitchens are often a big selling point to buyers. Investing in remodels that make the kitchen more spacious and usable will probably add significant value to the home. But don't think that because you just love ornate and colorful art deco tile in every available nook that the next owner will too. Digging up the yard and adding a pool may be an addition that you will enjoy, but keep in mind that buyers might miss the yard, have children for whom the pool is a risk, or be nervous about the extra costs and maintenance responsibilities. Make sure that your improvements improve your quality of life while at the same time enhancing the value of your home. It doesn't make sense to remodel your entire home and then sell it, denying yourself the chance to enjoy the improvements. Why not do enduring improvements over the years so that you can enjoy them as you live in the home? You can never guarantee that a single improvement will add value at resale, but at least you will have thoroughly enjoyed it. And, if you have made a steady stream of improvements over the years, then you can be fairly sure that you have added significant value to the property and that, over all, the effort and expenses will have paid off.

With your primary residence, slow and steady improvement done with an eye toward longevity is the smart way to go. However, if you are buying an investment property to rent out or sell, you can't afford to wait. Your refurbishment plan must match the intentions you have for the property. If you are buying a fixer upper and you plan to do a quick turn around, you need to determine what level of refurbishment will leave you with the best profit margin. Some improvements will not be worth the cost or effort involved.

Generally speaking, you want to bring the property up to speed with prevailing neighborhood standards. You may be tempted to try to make tempting improvements that would greatly increase the amount for which you can resell the property, but remember that the house's market price, the price for which it will be officially appraised, will not rise much above the level of other similarly sized houses in the area. So, you don't want to do expensive changes like installing granite countertops and top of the line wood floors in a house where the home values are quite moderate. These luxury improvements might make your house more desirable in a buyer's market, but they won't significantly boost the price you can expect. Instead, make improvements that transform the property into a well-groomed and clean property in visibly good repair. You want the prospective homeowner to be able to project their own dreams on the property. If they want Italian marble, they can install it. You have provided a sound, blank slate for their imagination. In this way you should be able to get fair market value for the home for which you have paid significantly less…and you have not poured unnecessary amounts of your profit into refurbishment.

In terms of income property, your refurbishment efforts need to be targeted toward longevity and easy maintenance. You may be able to get cheap materials that look good when someone is touring the property, but these will soon wear out and you will be replacing them every time you have a change in tenant, or sooner. Invest in simple, extremely durable materials when you prepare rental properties. Your tenants will appreciate that their linoleum isn't cracking and their fixtures aren't leaking as much as you will. Anticipate problems as you make design decisions in your properties. If the bathtub/shower is designed so that the water seems to pool on the edges and spill out onto the floor, this could be disastrous over time in terms of water damage and mold. The extra cost of installing shower doors will save you thousands in the long run. Keep an eye out for the future when refurbishing income property. And maintain, maintain, maintain! You know the old story about an ounce of prevention.

If you are interested in buying fairly dilapidated homes and then fixing them up for a quick sale or to rent out, then I have some tips for you:

Make sure that each improvement will net at least double the cost investment at resale. Otherwise, it is not worth it.

Do put a lot of effort into inexpensive cosmetic changes.

Do basic repairs that will make the space functional.

Do it quick—a vacant property is a money vacuum.

Generally, it is advisable to purchase a home that requires a fair amount of "sweat equity" and a low amount of financial investment. Whether or not you want to sweat yourself, or have someone else do it for you is entirely up to you and your style. Many real estate investors get into the business because they enjoy working on homes and can do work quickly and inexpensively. As their real estate portfolio grows, they may have less time to do things on their own and more money to hire things done. Look at the refurbishment needs of the home in terms of your profit margin and the strict budget you have for yourself.

One home may look terrible—dirty, walls that are scratched and gouged, cabinets hanging from their hinges—while another may look great but have hidden problems like plumbing or electrical in need of replacement. You can get the ugly duckling up to speed much more inexpensively than the good-looking one with hidden problems, but most buyers are more affected by the emotional impact of the visual problems. That is how you get the good deals. Hiring someone to clean and paint for two days will likely cost less than what a plumber or an electrician would charge for just a couple of hours worth of work.

Appliances

For an investment property, you generally don't want to invest in expensive new appliances; it will cut into your profits. If you are selling, buyers often expect to have to buy some of their own appliances, so if an appliance is missing or not in running order you may want to just let that be a feature of the property. If there is an appliance that doesn't work, don't leave it there in hopes its lack of functionality won't be noticed. Haul it away and carefully clean out the area in which it formerly resided. You can present the space as a positive for the buyer: "And it's all ready for the brand new stove of your choice," or "Here is where your washer and dryer will go!" That space leaves a better impression than an old stove that leaves the buyers fiddling with the knobs in frustration or a dryer that creates an eerie squeaking sound when turned on.

If you are getting the place ready to rent, it is better to have appliances there. Most renters don't have their own appliances, and this could be a deal breaker for many. If you have a lot of properties you may want to have a warehouse or garage somewhere where you have a store of functional appliances that you have saved from upgrades to other properties, auction sales, or second hand stores. You can find excellent deals in the classified ads. For a rental, the appliances don't need to be top of the line; they just need to be clean and functional. Don't go overboard on the number of appliances in a rental property, however. The more appliances that you provide, the more breakdowns can occur for which you are accountable. Just provide the basics. If they want a trash compactor and a microwave oven, they can bring them in.

Curb Appeal

Many buyers make up their minds tentatively about a property as they are driving up. The rest of the tour only serves to confirm or contradict their initial impression. If they drive up and their heart sinks as their eyes recoil from the sight of the paint peeling off the door and the unkempt hedges creeping up under the windows, it will take a great deal to get them to change their minds on the rest of the visit, if they even enter the place at all. Most buyers have a deep emotional invest-ment in the house hunt. They have a picket fence image of their future home and if you can convey that image, you have gone a long way toward a sale. For that reason, it is very important to judge how a prop-erty appears from the outside.

Luckily, most curb appeal fix-ups are relatively inexpensive. Get your lawnmower, weedwacker and hedge trimmer out and stand across the street to see how to give your property a facelift. First of all give the front a good cleaning and a good trimming. Remove all trash, mow, clip hedges, pull weeds, get the grass out of the cracks in the sidewalk. Then you can really see how the front of the house looks. While you probably don't want to paint the entire house, see if there are areas that are peeling and worn away. It may be worth your while to paint the trim and maybe the front door. The front door is a feature that has a great psychological affect on a buyer. It reflects upon both appearances and security. It doesn't matter that a door locks just as securely with the old paint than with a new one—a shiny new door just feels more comforting and secure to a homebuyer. If the exterior paint is really in bad shape, it may be worth your while to paint the entire house. Throw a scraping party—this will be the most time consuming part of the job. Pizza and beer and good company can go a long way in the procurement of free labor. Then the gallons of exterior paint that you will need to buy won't be such a huge investment. People care a great deal about how they are viewed by their neighbors, so improvements to the exterior are usually worth your while.

You may also want to invest in some inexpensive beautifiers that help solidify this emotional first reaction. Place some hanging baskets brimming with colorful flowers on the front porch—that will run you about $40. Shutters are not that expensive, but give a harsh exterior a softer, more charming appearance. Plant some bedding flowers along the front walk. Don't go crazy with expensive landscaping, just make sure that when you stand back, the front of the house looks clean, neat and welcoming. The backyard is important too, but less so. They've probably already made up their mind when they reach the backyard. Just make sure it is also mowed and trimmed and free of garbage. If there is an ugly storage shed in terrible condition, full of junk and old wood, harboring any number of critters, why not tear it down? A serious do it yourself real estate investor probably owns an old hauling truck and has a clean-up assistant on call who will load it up and drive it out to the dump for a small fee.

Cleaning

A dirty property is a real estate investor's best asset because it drives other buyers away, drives the price down and is an easy fix. What's a few grubby cabinets, stained walls, trash in the basement to you? I mentioned that real estate investing is not a glamorous profession, didn't I? There is really no cleaning challenge that cannot be addressed fairly easily with a good set of rubber gloves, some heavy duty cleaning solutions, and some good old fashioned scrubbing. Of course, you can have the property cleaned professionally to give you time to go out looking for other properties, or you can do it yourself. As you are cleaning, pretend that you yourself will be moving into the house. If you are a sloppy bachelor, bring a lady friend or your mother to the house. She will remind you that cleaning around the faucet handles with a toothbrush will go a long way toward subconsciously reassuring a potential buyer that she and her family will be safe and happy there. Get everything clean and sanitized and haul all the junk off the property.

Cosmetics

Once the interior is clean and bare, you can do inexpensive cosmetic work that will work wonders on the property. In such a case, paint is your best friend. Choose light colors. White will work, but people these days tend to think of light colors as warm and acceptable neutrals, so you may want to consider a very light sage green, yellow, cream or taupe to reduce the starkness of the empty space. Try to choose colors that would appeal to the widest cross section of people. If you have a large number of properties, you may want to choose a color to paint all your properties, such as white or cream. That way, you can buy paint in bulk, keep unused paint in your warehouse or garage to do patch work. It is less wasteful and saves you having to keep track of which colors you painted in which property. If the walls are in bad shape, this problem can be taken care of with a little spackle or joint compound, or even wallpaper (in a very neutral pattern).

Nothing turns people off more than dirty, smelly carpet. However, floor coverings can be expensive. If you are selling the property, choose a carpet that has an emotional impact. Picture a baby crawling on it—plush cream colored carpet often does the trick. If you are renting, select a durable, multicolored, preferably Berber style carpet that can take a lot of wear and tear and that will not show staining or traffic marks. Anytime you are renting a property out, durability must be your number one concern.

Especially when you are just starting out, your ability to do rehabilitations, inexpensively, effectively and quickly will have a lot to do with your cash flow. Later, as you have a diverse portfolio and a nice cushion, you can buy a plain property in highly desirable area and turn it into a luxury property, but for now think simple, cheap and fast.

9

No Real Estate Investor is an Island: The Professionals You'll Need to Get to Know

The real estate business can be pretty complicated: escrow, wrap-around mortgages, balloon mortgages, tax law, interest rates and inflation…it can all be a bit overwhelming. While you need to be involved in every step of your investment process to make sure that you are not being fleeced, you also must rely on the know-how of professionals, especially at the outset. The more experienced you become as a real estate investor, the more you can do on your own, but learn from the best, and educate yourself so that you can fully understand and verify the advice you are getting from your support professionals. As you build up your investments gradually, you will learn what you need to know. These are the professionals that you will need to lean on at the beginning, depending upon how complicated your investment strategy is: (If you are simply buying an additional home to rent out, you won't need quite the arsenal of professionals as you would if you were buying an office building or an apartment building, for example. The more your real estate investment portfolio grows, the more professional assistance you will most likely need.)

Real Estate Agents

When looking for a real estate agent, be very careful in your selection process. There is a great deal of difference between a real estate agent and a *good* real estate agent. Don't just open up a phone book and dial the first one on the list, requesting "an agent." The best way to find a good agent is to ask around. Find friends, colleagues, or family members who have recently bought a house in the neighborhood in which you want to buy. Ask them if they recommend their real estate agent. Only call that agent if they come "highly recommended." Ask your informant the following questions to assure that you will get the real estate agent that you need and deserve:

Did the agent set up an initial meeting to discuss your housing needs and desires?

Did the agent make him or herself available on multiple days at convenient times?

How many houses did the agent show you?

Was it easy to get in touch with your agent?

How did the agent respond if you didn't seem to like a house? (Did they view this as a valuable opportunity to more fully understand what you need in a house, or did they try to sell you on the house, ignoring your objections?)

Did the agent seem to do a "hard sell" on certain properties, or did he or she act as more of a "tour guide" and let you make your own judgments?

Did the agent seem knowledgeable about each house and the features of the house?

Did the agent show you any houses that had "just come on the market?" (Indicating that they are helping you to get a jump on the competition and that they are keeping their finger on the pulse of the market on your behalf.)

Did the agent stick with you through to the closing, helping you with needs ranging from procuring a key, having the house inspected, and communicating with the seller as needed?

A good reference is an important aspect of finding a good real estate agent, but there are other things to consider as well. For instance, how long has your agent been practicing? And how long in the same area? In the business of real estate, experience matters a great deal. The longer a real estate agent has worked in the area, the more connections he or she has made, the more knowledge he or she has of houses, the market and the area. You don't want to have an agent who is brand new or has just moved to the area and may not have the resources and knowledge necessary to find you the very best house for your needs. Real estate is an industry in which experience counts.

If you are on the purchasing end of the transaction, it is crucial to make sure that your agent is representing you as a *buyer's agent*. This means that he or she is representing *you* in the transaction and does not have loyalties divided between you and the seller. You want assure that your agent will not be providing information to the seller that will hurt your chances of getting the best possible deal. Do not deal directly with the *seller's agent* who has listed the house. By law, a *buyer's agent* cannot betray your interests for the benefit of the seller. Remember, both agents in the transaction are making a commission. Your agent should not be running to the seller's agent saying, "My client is going to offer $180,000, but he said he is willing to go up to $200,000." Still, you cannot ever be sure of what is happening outside of your knowledge, so even if you have a great real estate agent, don't tell them how high you will go. In fact, try to give the impression that you could take or leave the property and that you have given the price you are willing to pay. You can always come back with a higher counter-offer if you desire, but you don't have to advertise your willingness to do so. Hold your cards in close, even with a trusted agent. This is business!

Do You Actually Need a Real Estate Agent?

This is a complicated and personal decision. It has much to do with your personality, your investing style, and the extent of your real estate investing career aspirations. Most full time real estate investors that I know use real estate agents some of the time; they certainly have strong connections with at least one real estate agent. However, they also know the value of bypassing the large sales commission, selling their properties on their own and dealing with "For Sale By Owner." Sellers.

A good real estate agent does know the business inside and out and that knowledge can be helpful to you. This professional knows the business and the local market inside and out. Some advantages of using a real estate agent:

They save you time. You are, after all, paying them for *doing* something. They take care of a great deal of paperwork for you, they look for properties that might suit your needs, and they communicate with the sellers.

The have access to a lot of information. They know the market and they know the area, but chances are most seasoned real estate investors do too. However, licensed real estate agents have access to MLS listings and databases that may not be available to unlicensed investors. They also have computer programs that allow them to search for and filter information that would take you a great deal of time to sift through.

They know the procedures that will protect you and keep things legal. If you are an inexperienced investor you may skip an important step in the paperwork trail or neglect to take a step to protect yourself in the transaction. Of course, whether or not you hire an agent, you need an attorney to see you through the deal, and they should be able to offer you some protection. As a real estate investor, it will be your responsibility to know how to execute a solid real estate deal.

Of course, there are also some disadvantages that come along with using a real estate agent:

They are expensive. Of course, the biggest downside to using a real estate agent is, of course, *cost*. The first rule of investing is to pay the lowest price for a property and make the highest profit. The six to eight percent commission the agent makes will probably come out of your profit.

They can sometimes get in the way. Anyone who has used an agent during a sale or a purchase will notice that they prefer that you don't get very involved in the negotiations process. In fact, most real estate agents prefer that their clients don't even meet the opposing party until closing. If you are a savvy investor who uses creativity in deal-making and who has excellent skills of negotiation, the real estate agent could be limiting your effectiveness.

Real estate agents can sometimes slow down the process. Agents have certain processes and legal requirements that they need to fulfill. Real estate investing is a game that requires excellent timing and agents can sometimes gum up the works and slow things down.

The bottom line is that real estate agents have a great deal to offer, but successful real estate investors learn to minimize their reliance upon them.

Some real estate investors decide to get their own real estate licenses. This can be smart as the licensing process will provide you with good information about real estate law and transaction procedures, and you will gain access to information that is harder to get as a non licensed investor. However, being a dual investor/agent has its downsides too. As an agent you will have different disclosure requirements during the transaction process that may complicate your sale. Also, some people are less likely to feel comfortable dealing with an agent/investor and may not understand your dual purpose.

An Accountant

As a real estate investor, you will absolutely need one of these. A good real estate investor will be consulting with his or her accountant continually. The accountant can do the calculations necessary to really determine if a property will generate a good return. An accountant can foresee problems with cash flow and can negotiate you through the ever-changing tax laws. There are accountants that specialize in real estate. Make sure you like your accountant, because you will have a long relationship with frequent contact.

An Attorney

You may not need an attorney's help on a regular basis or with every real estate deal, but you should have one to consult with if you are concerned or unsure about a contract or have a special situation that concerns you. Most real estate investors have an attorney at the ready that they consult with on an occasional basis. Many others rely more heavily upon an attorney, running each and every contract and legal document by their attorney to build a rock solid assurance that there will be no unexpected legal ramifications with which to contend. Attorney's can help you set up a partnership deal, draw up leases and contracts, and help you with sticky tenant situations such as evictions. An attorney's help can be invaluable because they help keep you on the right side of the law and protect your interests in the various agreements you will make. However, be careful that you do not make use of an attorney's services too lightly or too liberally. They charge exorbitant hourly fees and those fees begin the minute that they pick up the phone to talk with you. So, for example, you might want to simply purchase a boilerplate contract for an agreement, but then pay for the attorney to just look it over briefly to approve it, rather than having the attorney take the time to draw up all of your contracts for you. After a while, you will gain confidence about your transactions and you will gain an understanding of real estate law and will rely less upon your attorney. On the other hand, the more complicated and numerous your investing strategies become, the more likely you may need the help of an attorney. Of course, by that time you'll be able to afford one!

A Banker

Whenever you are about to make a real estate transaction, there is one professional that stands in your way. He or she must determine if your transaction is a good risk and whether you will be successful in your endeavor to pay your mortgage. If you have a banker that has witnessed your past successes, your level of knowledge, seriousness and professionalism, then you will have a much smoother journey as you make each of your investments. Since competition is always good for the consumer, you may want to cultivate good relationships with several bankers. If you need a loan in a hurry to capitalize on a good deal, you will have several from which to choose. It is advisable to create a good impression when getting to know your neighborhood bankers. You want to build the impression that you run a solid and reliable investment business and that you are always a good risk. The more confident they are in you, the more quickly your transaction will be completed.

An Appraiser

When you need to make sure that your property is priced at or below market, the only way to make sure is to hire an appraiser to inspect the property. This is information that you can bring to the bank—literally!

A Title Company

A title company is a necessary component of the closing process. They will look up the title on the property and provide a report of any debts or liens there are against the property. This is an important protection for a buyer, because if you purchase a property and there is an outstanding debt or lien against that property, the new owner becomes responsible. You want to be sure that all such entanglements are taken care of before you buy a property. If you don't use a real estate agent, the title company will arrange and execute the closing. Using a good title company is a little bit like having an accountant, an attorney and a real estate agent all at your disposal for a much reduced price. They are very familiar with the processes of real estate transactions and they can answer most of your questions, lead you through the process, and protect you from your own ignorance.

A Property Management Company

For successful investors who don't enjoy the position of landlord, hiring a management company to take care of your property can be a good idea. After all, doing it all yourself really limits the amount of rental properties you can own. Being a landlord for just a couple of small apartment buildings can be a full time job. For a fee, a property management company will prepare and rent out vacant units, do routine repairs and maintenance, collect rents, and handle all tenant communications. However, in order to protect your investment, it is always advisable to stay very involved in your properties even if you hire a management company. Regularly tour the properties, insist upon being advised about every transaction, and keep your eye on the books, or better yet, have your accountant regularly review all of the expenditures and earnings on the property. Beginning investors usually manage their own properties, but management companies can allow real estate investors to really expand their holdings beyond what they could reasonably manage on their own.

The All Important Home Inspector

After you have selected a property, you can start the mortgage application process, but don't get too attached. Get a home inspector to come and check out the place as soon as possible. You have the right to pull out of the deal if the inspector uncovers defects in the home that will be of significant cost to you. (The exact dollar amount varies by state.) So, if you have found your perfect house, but the home inspector reveals that the foundation is crumbling, you can still, and should, move on. One of the biggest mistakes real estate investors make is not hiring an inspector in order to save money. The buyer may have felt he was "handy" and could spot any trouble. But does he own a device that can detect gas leaks? Does he specialize in plumbing, electric, structural engineering and roofing? A true "handyperson" recognizes the necessity of a professional inspection. I know professionals in the construction industry that still hire home inspectors when buying a property.

Sometimes people neglect to hire a home inspector because the home they are buying is new, or at least relatively new. Only older homes have problems, right? Absolutely wrong. The older homes have at least shown the test of time. While they may be in more need of replacement updates, the original work on an older home has been proven. Many people argue that building materials and cost-cutting methods in new cookie cutter developments are not what they used to be. You need to assure that the work that has been done on a house has been done correctly, especially since the home has not yet been asked the stand the test of time.

The home inspector will give you a detailed report that you can use as a reference if you forget the details that you have learned about the home. It should tell you what kind of roof you have and how long it has been up there. It will tell you how old your boiler is and what type it is, and so on. Be sure to be there for the inspection and ask lots of questions. Take notes. From a good inspector, you can learn about the upkeep and maintenance needs of your house. You want an inspector who welcomes you at his side as he works, and who is talkative, giving you a running commentary of his observations. (It is a good idea to get a recommendation on a house inspector as well. Often your real estate agent knows a good inspector.) If the inspector discovers something that is a safety hazard, it is generally up to the seller to fix it before you take possession of the house. Otherwise, you have to decide if the costs associated with the property are ones you are willing to take on. If the costs reach a certain level, (which varies from state to state) you are entitled to back out of the deal. You may decide to still take on the property, but at least you will have made an informed decision. You may also want to ask your inspector to do a radon test if radon is an issue in your area. If the radon level comes up high, the seller may have to have it mitigated before you move in.

After you have been approved for your mortgage and are headed toward a triumphant closing, don't forget one last detail. Schedule a pre-closing inspection. I can't tell you how many stories I have heard about people skipping this step and ending up regretting it. At the pre-closing inspection, you want to be sure that the house is still in the condition that it was at the first inspection. "Surprise! There was a kitchen fire since you saw the house last." You also want to be sure that all of the agreed upon inclusions are still there. "Surprise! The owner decided to rip out all those original light fixtures and leave instead ragged gaps in the ceiling with wires dangling down." A pre-closing inspection will assure that there are "no surprises" when you take ownership of the house.

As a real estate investor, over the years you will cultivate close working relationships with a wide variety of professionals. Others will include **insurance agents, construction professionals, landscapers, wholesalers (for buying materials), plumbers, electricians**…the list goes on. You will probably also benefit greatly from having your own trusted "handyman" (or woman) on call for all the little jobs you don't have the time or skill to attend to yourself. The most successful real estate investors have a wide arsenal of people that they trust, that they have a long history of doing business with and upon whom they are sure they can rely.

All of these professionals, once long term associates and friends, can also provide valuable informal services—they can let you know about properties that they have encountered, give you back stories on sellers and property conditions, point you toward the best deals on materials and services, and so on. Of course, you will do the same for them and their particular business concerns. This is the power of the kind of business network that you cultivate over the years. For the real estate investor, relationships are very important.

10

The Sky's the Limit

If the prospect of investing in real estate is new to you, perhaps you haven't even purchased your first home yet, then your head may be spinning right now. Property management firms? Hiring an accountant? Lease options? There really are a lot of new challenges that you will encounter if you choose to take this journey. But now is not the time to unduly worry about all the details. This book is an overview, and right now an overview is all you need. If you are starting out, it is important to start small, focus on one step in the process at a time, and feel confident that you can learn what you need to know as you go along. In my case, each time I face a new challenge the first thing I do is buy a book about it or head down to the public library. If you try to learn everything at once, you will become overwhelmed and lose your confidence.

For those of us who are struggling financially and really need to make a bold move to overcome financial obstacles and cross over into the worlds of security and abundance, confidence and optimism are the two most important qualities that you can have on your side. These are much more important than a degree in economics or a hard driving business personality. Confidence and optimism. You maintain these by focusing on each step in your journey. Your first step may be taking some preliminary measures to improve your credit. Or, it could be that you need to save up a few thousand dollars to invest in your first income property. Maybe you already have the money and are ready for the fun task of hunting for a bargain property. Wherever you are, focus your attention there, and don't plan or worry too far into the future.

Real estate investing works step-by-step, building block-by-block. You won't become a land baron overnight, despite the claims of some of the real estate hucksters selling you videotapes on TV.

But it does work. Sometimes real lived experience is better than a thousand words of encouragement or advice, however, so let me tell you what happened next in the story of Eric and Mya…you know the couple who bought a foreclosed house after Mya was injured?…the couple who moved from the campground directly into their new home despite being completely destitute? Well, I sat down recently with Mya and talked to her about her new career direction.

Mya and Eric are doing well in their new house. They got such a bargain, that once Eric got promoted several times in his agency, making the mortgage payment was a piece of cake for them. While recovering from her injury, Mya befriended the family next door. She lent a sympathetic ear as the family started having financial trouble and the husband and wife finally determined that they would divorce. The husband moved out, and Mya looked on while the remaining spouse tried and tried to sell the house, which was in pretty bad shape. Mya started secretly doing some reading…and some saving. When she had $2,500 in her bank account, she was ready to make an offer on her neighbor's house. She got it for a steal at $50,000, and her neighbor was nothing but grateful. Now Mya and Eric owned two properties, side by side. The two got busy reversing the neglect on the house next door, and quickly rented it out at $750 a month. They pay only $550 in payments on the house, which leaves them with a $200 a month positive cash flow on the property. The really wonderful news is that Mya recently had the house appraised at $68,000 dollars! If they sold it tomorrow they would have $18,000 sitting in their savings account, making money for their future. However, I think Eric and Mya will hold on to this gem of an investment and let appreciation do a little more for their net worth. After all, the city sprawl is reaching out toward their rural area, and before you know it, busy professional families working in the city will be yearning for a nice country retreat within easy commuting distance. You can bet that Mya has her eye open for other distressed properties in the area. And just a couple of years prior, this couple was homeless and destitute.

Real estate has the power to change the lives of *real* people. Many people who would really benefit from real estate don't get involved because they don't see the potential in themselves. They believe that wealth is only for the highly educated or those born into it. The best they hope for is a promotion to manager at their current job. This puts a definitive cap on their future dreams. They lack the confidence and the information that could allow them to harness the democratic wealth building strategy of real estate investing. But there are people out there like Eric and Mya who aren't going to allow their current situation to place limits upon their future.

Are you one of them? What do you need to do today to get started in real estate investing?

11

Using the Power of eBay

In the past most real estate investors had to be satisfied with the opportunities presented locally. In some cases, an investor could drive a couple of hours and look at properties in a nearby city.

But for the most part real estate entrepreneurs have been confined to their geographical area.

With the advent of the real estate category on eBay an entrepreneur can search, buy, and sell properties that are located through out the world. When using eBay it is important that caution should be used, and that you should not fall into the trap of buying property sight unseen.

Make sure to apply everything you have learned in this book when using eBay to invest in real estate.

There are many sub categories on eBay such as land, residential, commercial, and foreclosure listings. You can also run a more detailed search by inputting the exact search criteria that you are looking for.

The true benefit of using eBay to invest in real estate, whether as a buyer or seller, is that you can instantly expand your focus on a global basis. All of the same rules apply but now the playing field has been greatly expanded.

One of the interesting opportunities that are created by eBay is the matching up of buyers and sellers. In the past, if a seller wanted to sell a former post office in a rural village, there was little the seller could do.

But today that same seller can connect with a software developer looking for a cheaper building to expand into. These two parties would never have met, or considered the alternate use for the property if it was not for eBay.

So as you can see, it is very important to realize that eBay can be used to market a property based on an alternate need that local residents might not have. In other words, there might be a very eager buyer for your property if you can show him or her how the property can serve their purposes.

The same is true in the reverse. Many times you will see a property being sold on eBay for a very low price. There is a chance that the price is so low simply because the seller cannot imagine alternate uses for that property. If you can think of a creative use for that property you can buy it on eBay and then start marketing it according to the use you envision for it.

You can even use what you have learned to buy and sell property on eBay. You can buy a property, upgrade it, and then re list it on eBay for a handsome profit.

The possibilities for you to make money on real estate using eBay are limited only by your imagination.

0-595-34496-8

www.ingramcontent.com/pod-product-compliance
Lightning Source LLC
Chambersburg PA
CBHW030858180526
45163CB00004B/1626